So Send I You

So Send I You

God's Progress of Redemption: Part Two

Rod Culbertson

WIPF & STOCK · Eugene, Oregon

SO SEND I YOU
God's Progress of Redemption: Part Two

Copyright © 2019 Rod Culbertson. All rights reserved. Except for brief quotations in critical publications or reviews, no part of this book may be reproduced in any manner without prior written permission from the publisher. Write: Permissions, Wipf and Stock Publishers, 199 W. 8th Ave., Suite 3, Eugene, OR 97401.

Wipf & Stock
An Imprint of Wipf and Stock Publishers
199 W. 8th Ave., Suite 3
Eugene, OR 97401

www.wipfandstock.com

PAPERBACK ISBN: 978-1-5326-6834-0
HARDCOVER ISBN: 978-1-5326-6835-7
EBOOK ISBN: 978-1-5326-6836-4

Manufactured in the U.S.A.   APRIL 8, 2019

Unless otherwise indicated, all Scripture quotations are from The Holy Bible, English Standard Version® (ESV®), copyright © 2001 by Crossway, a publishing ministry of Good News Publishers. Used by permission. All rights reserved.

Dedication

I WISH TO DEDICATE this book to the late Dr. Will Norton, former professor of almost everything at the Charlotte campus of Reformed Theological Seminary. If there is anyone who embodied the calling of our Lord Jesus Christ to follow him anywhere, and to respond to the Great Commission, it was Will Norton, along with his lovely, dedicated, and godly wife, Colene.

Dr. Norton graduated from Wheaton College in 1936, and then enrolled at the recently established graduate school of Columbia Bible College (now Columbia International University) where, along with Dr. Robert C. McQuilkin, he helped start the Student Foreign Missions Fellowship (SFMF). Interestingly, Dr. Norton was one of the first three graduates from CIU's graduate school, along with none other than James "Buck" Hatch, the professor who taught me the "Progress of Redemption" course there. After finishing at CIU, he and Colene served as missionaries in the Belgian Congo, and in 1946 he helped start the first InterVarsity Missions conference eventually known as Urbana. In time, he served as president at Trinity College and Trinity Evangelical Divinity School. In 1965 Dr. Norton joined the faculty of Wheaton College Graduate School and eventually became the dean, helping to start the Wheaton Graduate School program in missions. He was Professor of Missions at Reformed Theological Seminary in Jackson, Mississippi and in his final (and fourth) retirement, he became the Distinguished Professor of Missions at Reformed Theological Seminary in Charlotte. He also founded two seminaries in Africa in order to provide theological training for those who could not leave their countries for traditional, residential seminary training. He passed away in 2017 at the blessed age of 102.

Some years ago I did some research and discovered that Dr. Norton taught the following courses in the early years of the Charlotte campus of Reformed Theological Seminary: Church History I and II, Evangelism, Missions, Classics of Personal Devotion, and Sanctification, along with three different missions electives (World Religions, Strategic Issues in Missions, and Revival and Global Missions). He was a very well educated and gifted man and could tackle many subjects. However, the thought that he left with the many students who listened to him lecture would be this: "In every course, he *only* talks about Luke chapter 24—how the disciples on the road to Emmaus had burning hearts while they listened to Jesus open the Old Testament Scriptures to show them how they testify of him!" His was a constant theme—walk with Jesus. On reflection, however, usually the students would say, "And that's what we need to hear to make it through ministry, i.e., to have hearts burning for Christ as we daily read our Bibles and walk with him."

So Send I You is dedicated to a man who was, in every way, sent by a savior whom he both knew and loved. I count it one of the great privileges of my life to have known Will Norton. May this book cause our hearts to burn for Christ as we read about how he sent and blessed his church in those early days, as recorded in the book of Acts.

Contents

Illustrations | ix
Preface | xi
Acknowledgements | xiii
Introduction | xv

Act Two | 1
    Step One: "The Seed" | 4
    Step Two: "Out" of Jerusalem | 19
    Step Three: "To The Gentiles" | 25
    Step Four: "The First True Church" | 33
    Step Five: "To The World" | 37
    Conclusion | 51

Appendix | 55
Bibliography | 75

Illustrations

Figure 1: Review | 6
Figure 2: The Seed Grows: Acts 1–2 | 9
Figure 3: The Seed Grows: Acts 2 | 10
Figure 4: Opposition/Persecution/Growth | 15
Figure 5: Persecution to Death | 18
Figure 6: "Out" of Jerusalem | 24
Figure 7: "To the Gentiles" | 32
Figure 8: "The First True Church" | 36
Figure 9: "To the World" | 50

Preface

So Send I You is a continuation of an earlier volume, *As The Father Has Sent Me*. Together, both books attempt to demonstrate how the biblical story of God's plan of redemption in the world graciously unfolds. *So Send I You* is the second of two books that summarize God's plan to redeem, or rescue, a people for himself for his own glory. *As The Father Has Sent Me* addressed the beginning of God's plan for the world as described in the book of Genesis, climaxing with the coming of Christ as the promised son of God (act one in God's redemptive plan). Jesus is sacrificed on the cross for the sins of his people; the message of his death and resurrection is the centerpiece of world history. In *As The Father Has Sent Me*, God's "drama of redemption" unfolds before our very eyes, as the channel of God's redemptive plan is provided through the building of the nation of Israel. Christ came to his own, but ultimately he had come to make himself known to the world! *So Send I You* continues the story of Christ's coming, a purpose with the entire world in mind. We will begin with Christ's command to his disciples to make other disciples (or followers) throughout the earth, and describe the early days of the growth and reproduction seen in the church of God (often against many impediments and obstacles). As you read *So Send I You*, you will watch God expand his saving acts, going beyond his beloved nation of Israel, desiring to show himself to the world whom he also loves, and as you read, you may discover that you are a part of God's story as well—yes, it could be true. I hope you will enjoy book two as the companion piece that completes the story. Let's rejoice in God's plan for us, and for his world, through the sending of his son Jesus, who sends us to proclaim his gospel everywhere.

Acknowledgements

IN MY PREVIOUS BOOK on the subject of God's progress of redemption, *As The Father Has Sent Me*, I acknowledged that the bulk of the work was a product of the instruction of Presbyterian minister, Reverend Mr. James "Buck" Hatch, Professor of Bible, among other things, at Columbia International University. This book, *So Send I You*, also consists of many of the notes from his insightful course, "Progress of Redemption," a course well known to most of the graduates of CIU in the sixties, seventies, eighties, nineties, and into the twenty-first-century. I have tried to recapture the New Testament portion of this course to some extent, and to further enhance it with many personal observations (and graphics) of my own.

Many thanks are due to my professional graphics artist for creating some very nice pictures that enhance this work. Kirby McCreight is a very gifted graphics man who provided both t-shirt graphics and logos while involved in my RUF ministry at the University of Florida in the eighties. He was gracious enough to provide his generous assistance for this book. I am very grateful to Christ for Kirby and his willingness to serve in this project.

I also must thank my teaching assistant at Reformed Theological Seminary, Ms. Anna Unkefer, who enables me to publish a book such as this one. I am deeply grateful for her work and diligence on my behalf. Finally, I appreciate one special reader who assisted me in editing this work and bringing clarity to my thoughts on paper: Mrs. Tari Williamson, long-time friend and Christian educator.

Introduction

Four hundred years of silence! That was the setting when God sent his son, Jesus, into the world. We can hardly imagine such silence on the part of a God who made us with a desire to know him. Even in our world today, we can barely go forty seconds without sound or some sort of communication. Yet, the Lord is so exacerbated with his people, the nation of Israel, that he stops speaking and acting. He sends no prophets to call them back to the way of godliness. He does no miracles or acts of providence on their behalf. Four hundred years without God intervening in some significant manner is quite unbelievable.

But God has a plan. It is a plan of redemption and salvation for his people. He is going to graciously rescue a portion of the rebellious from their fallenness and dilemma. Sinners are in peril. Yes, he has a plan for the world! In the book of Genesis, God promises Abraham that he will make of him (an elderly man with a barren wife, i.e., a childless couple) *a great nation*. That promise was fulfilled through the eventual building of a theocracy: a nation led by God through a man of God's choosing. And that theocracy was Israel. Yet, God makes a second promise to Abraham, one which contains assurance that he will bless *the entire world* through Abraham's seed (offspring). And in time, the Lord will indeed reach his goal for the earth: that all of "the earth will be filled with the knowledge of the glory of the LORD as the waters cover the sea!"[1]

However, a surprising circumstance in God's plan occurs. At the end of the Old Testament, the channel of God's redemption appears to have faded into insignificance. The nation of Israel has been living in bondage to a number of major world nations (Assyria, Babylon, Greece, and Rome) for a number of centuries. As a nation, their spiritual well-being has decayed in such a manner that, in the early first-century, most of their spiritual leaders are missing a heart for God and participating in lifeless and disingenuous

1. Hab 2:14.

Introduction

worship. The former theocracy is no longer living underneath God's kingship. Israel has become a nation with little true spirituality. A remnant does remain, one that awaits a promised messiah who will come and set them free from their captivity. The observer might well reason, "Who could have hope for any spiritual breakthrough after four hundred years of silence on God's part?" and "Will anything ever happen again in the life of God's chosen people?"

God Works

God does come; the gospels record the story. Jesus—God in the flesh—comes and shows us God's glory. Who is this Jesus and where has he come from? The gospels answer this question. Among the four gospel accounts of Jesus—Matthew, Mark, Luke, and John[2]—only two include genealogical literature, i.e., the tracing of Christ's origins. These are Matthew and Luke. The gospel of Mark is written to a Roman audience, is shorter in content and fast-paced in style (in order to maintain the attentiveness of the Roman reader), and thematically portrays Christ as a servant. Servants did not have birth certificates and often did not know their families of origin; therefore, Mark includes no genealogy. The gospel of John is written to a universal audience, i.e., a universal church consisting of both Jews and Gentiles. John's gospel presentation is unique and dissimilar to the other gospels in many ways. He does not include a genealogy in his account of Christ because he presents a picture of Christ in his highest essence, as the very Son of God. John declares that this Jesus, although coming to earth as a man in the flesh, is none other than God himself! The eternal God has stooped down to redeem his people. Declaring that Christ therefore has no beginning within time, John does not recount the Son of God's human lineage or genealogy. Christ is eternal.

Nevertheless, the gospels of Matthew and Luke include not only genealogical accounts of Christ, but brief stories surrounding the circumstances of his birth and childhood. Luke even tells a story of Jesus's boyhood with relation to temple worship. Matthew writes (for demonstration to his own people, the Jews—those who rejected Christ) that Jesus came to bring the long-awaited kingdom of God. Christ will rule over his people through a spiritual kingdom; thus Matthew portrays Christ as a king. He traces Jesus's

---

2. Not Fred (if you read previously *As The Father Has Sent Me*, you will understand this faux pas).

INTRODUCTION

genealogy from the most prominent king of Israel, King David. Luke writes to a Gentile audience, and as a converted Gentile himself, hopes that they will believe in Christ; thus he describes Christ as the one who came *as a man* to reach mankind! Luke begins his gospel with stories about the birth of both John the Baptist (Christ's forerunner, or "front man," so to speak) and Jesus. In chapter 3, after presenting these birth narratives, Luke traces Christ's lineage back to the first man, Adam. Christ is a man—an actual human being—who came to redeem mankind.

I mention the details of these four gospels and their themes (Matthew: Christ as a king, Mark: Christ as a servant, Luke: Christ as a man, and John: Christ as God) for a reason. Because when God is both speaking and acting, i.e., working in the most significant of ways, he deliberately underscores his work. And, in the case of sending Christ his son, he underscores this message *four* times! God, the Father, declares emphatically that he is sending his son into the world in order to reach the world. His son is the king of the universe, yet the servant of mankind. He is both a human in the flesh and God incarnate, an eternal deity humbling himself in loving condescension among humanity. God is working in the grandest of manners—he comes to us through the second person of the Trinity; the world needs to know both who he is and what he has done. Therefore, God the father provides us with four powerful gospel accounts.

The remainder of this book will focus upon the work of Christ's church as he commissions his disciples and pours out his Holy Spirit upon them. We will observe the message of the good news of forgiveness of sins as it cascades through God's people, beginning in Jerusalem before it pulsates over all the earth. Let's watch God work and realize that he wants the world to know his love.

Act Two

Background

PRIOR TO ACT ONE, the Bible begins with a prologue to the story of redemption. The first eleven chapters of Genesis provide an account demonstrating that though God has created all things as good, Adam and Eve's subsequent disobedience and moral fall in the garden of Eden has brought catastrophic consequences upon the face of the earth. Mankind is now fallen, and wherever people exist sin reigns. Adam's original sin is passed along to his sons, ending in the murder of one by the other. Eventually, "The Lord saw that the wickedness of man was great in the earth, and that every intention of the thoughts of his heart was only evil continually."[1] The world is destroyed by a consuming flood and when, in time, civilization and the population increase, the people decide to build a tower toward heaven as a monument to themselves, and as an act of rebellion toward God's command to spread his glory around the world. This "prologue" to the redemptive story demonstrates man's need for God's intervention. The prologue leads us to act one in God's story.

Act One Review

Scene One

Act one of God's redemptive plan consists of three basic parts: God calls Abram (soon to be renamed Abraham) and promises to bless him by making of him a great nation, and by using him to bless the entire world! The first promise—making a great nation from his offspring—requires a lengthy narrative, beginning in Genesis chapter 12 and continuing through the books of First and Second Samuel. God builds a redemptive channel

1. Gen 6:5.

by which people can know him; the pinnacle of that channel is seen in the reigns of King David and his son, Solomon. Israel becomes a theocracy (a nation ruled by God through a man of God's choosing), and at the height of this theocracy, we see a little bit of heaven on earth. As we summarize God's wonderful theocracy, we see this kingdom characterized by the following attributes: justice and righteousness, victory and dominion, peace and safety, wisdom, joy, and happiness. Furthermore, we see prosperity and wealth, the temple and the worship of God, the presence of the glory of God in the temple, nations seeking to see the glory of the king, and sacrifices that provide assurance of atonement for sins, as well as forgiveness and salvation. Now seems like a good time to send Jesus, but that is not God's plan. His thoughts are higher than our thoughts and his ways are higher than our ways.

Scene Two

Due to King Solomon's love for his many foreign wives, and his ensuing idolatry and unfaithfulness, God begins to destroy his channel of redemption: the kingdom of Israel. Firstly, he splits the kingdom into a northern portion (still called Israel) and a southern portion (called Judah). Secondly, because the nation of Israel (the northern kingdom) perpetually engages in both false worship and idolatrous pagan practices (often led by their own kings) God destroys it. He raises up the great Assyrian empire which attacks and conquers the northern kingdom. Israel is destroyed (this event is crisis A). Thirdly, although it takes much longer (over one hundred years longer), the southern kingdom—Judah—also falls into a pagan idolatry so great that God promises to wipe them away like a person wipes a dish, utterly removing all evidence of filth on the plate. God ordains the nation of Babylon to ominously swoop down and sweep away not only the remaining kingdom of Judah, but to destroy both Jerusalem (*the place* for meeting God) and the temple, God's holy dwelling place. God's glory departs from his people as they are dragged away as slaves, living in a state of humiliation throughout the Babylonian empire (this event is crisis B).

The captivity of God's people among blatant pagans continues for seventy years. God's discipline for idolatry is harsh, severe, necessary, and understandable.

ACT TWO

Scene Three

God demonstrates his grace to his people—whom he has disciplined—when he raises up a foreign king, Cyrus of the Medo-Persian Empire, to restore them. Cyrus decrees that the shamed and enslaved people of God can return to their homeland to rebuild the temple. They return in stages, reconstructing the temple, restoring worship and the law of God to the reestablished nation (through Ezra), and repairing/building a wall of security around the city of Jerusalem (through Nehemiah). The redemptive channel of God, although a far cry from its previous glory under Kings David and Solomon (making this event crisis C), is now reestablished. However, God's glory does not return to the temple, nor are the remaining captives bold enough to approach God or mention his name in their scattered enslavement (Esther). Although restored to their land, the people of God, in time, fall back into ungodliness and disobedience; God sends them one last rebuke for their disingenuous worship and giving, compromised lifestyles, as well as their overall dishonoring of him (Malachi).

God then ceases to speak, act, or reveal himself for an unfathomable period of four hundred years. Four hundred years of silence—until, in the perfect time, God sends his son, born of a woman and born under the law, to redeem and adopt his chosen people (Gal 4:4–5). So great is this matter of God both acting and speaking that he gives us four distinct gospel accounts—four exclamation points—saying, "This is my beloved Son; listen to him!!!!" (Mark 9:7)

Changing His Channel

As we move from act one to act two, something major changes. What God is doing has changed—God's channel of redemption has changed. In act one, God is building *a nation*, a covenant community of people organized nationally, through which he will send his son, the messiah and redeemer of his people. In act two, God uses the New Testament expression of his church to make the news of his great work at the cross known to *the nations*. From one nation to many nations, God is working in order to reach his goal: "All the earth shall be filled with the knowledge of the glory of God" (Hab 2:14). The book of Acts is rightly named, as when we read it, we are watching the acts of God (or the acts of the Holy Spirit through Christ's apostles) in the context of the changing of the channel. Acts, chapters 1–12, describes the transition of the channel from the church, as one nation, to the church *for* the nations.

Step One: "The Seed"

IN MATTHEW 16:13–19, WE find this conversation between Jesus and his disciples:

> 13 Now when Jesus came into the district of Caesarea Philippi, he asked his disciples, "Who do people say that the Son of Man is?" 14 And they said, "Some say John the Baptist, others say Elijah, and others Jeremiah or one of the prophets." 15 He said to them, "But who do you say that I am?" 16 Simon Peter replied, "You are the Christ, the Son of the living God." 17 And Jesus answered him, "Blessed are you, Simon Bar-Jonah! For flesh and blood has not revealed this to you, but my Father who is in heaven. 18 And I tell you, you are Peter, and on this rock I will build my church, and the gates of hell shall not prevail against it. 19 I will give you the keys of the kingdom of heaven, and whatever you bind on earth shall be bound in heaven, and whatever you loose on earth shall be loosed in heaven.

The first three verses of this passage (13–15) are related to act one of God's progressive drama of redemption. The people of Israel are looking for their messiah. The masses always have opinions and conjectures about current events, and Jesus explores the thoughts of his very own, intimate followers. The conclusions of the masses, as stated by Jesus's disciples, are varied, but are not sheer speculation. At least they are trying to figure out who Jesus might be, and their guesses are formed on the basis of Old Testament knowledge. Nevertheless, Jesus penetrates further into the understanding of his disciples—the inner circle—wanting to inquire about their own conclusions. What happens next is a statement for the ages.

In verse 16, Peter, the usual spokesman for the twelve, emphatically declares, "You are the Christ, the Son of the living God." This profession is recorded elsewhere in the gospels in a more truncated fashion (Mark 8:29). However, the three inclusions of the word "the" in the confession provide

Step One: "The Seed"

the most forceful declaration possible. "You are *the* Christ, *the* Son of *the* living God" (emphasis mine). Christ is the messiah. Inexplicably, Peter summarizes the entire goal of act one. God, the Father, has sent his son to be *the* messiah of the world! However, he doesn't fully understand what he is saying, nor is this statement a product of his own thinking. Jesus reminds Peter (and the other disciples, I'm sure) that Peter's statement is not gleaned from his own insight. A confession as discerning as this one is only known or spoken through the gracious revelation of the Father.

In verse 18, Jesus then makes a second stunning revelation. He says to Peter, "And I tell you, you are Peter, and on this rock *I will build my church*, and the gates of hell shall not prevail against it" (italics mine for emphasis). In one short utterance, Jesus proposes the plan of act two in God's progress of redemption. The "rock" is the confession, not Peter himself. Nevertheless, the confession represents both Peter and this motley band of followers. Together, they will be the foundation of God's work in act two. Christ will build his church upon the rock of Peter's confession, as well as upon the foundation of these disciples' doctrine, i.e., their belief in Christ's messiahship. Peter, as the spokesman of the twelve disciples, is stating that to which these twelve men have given their lives. They believe that Christ is the promised savior from God. This is *the seed promise* for act two.

Do you remember the "seed" promise God made to Abram (Abraham)?

> Now the Lord said to Abram, "Go from your country and your kindred and your father's house to the land that I will show you. 2 And *I will make of you a great nation*, and I will bless you and make your name great, so that you will be a blessing. 3 I will bless those who bless you, and him who dishonors you I will curse, and in you all the families of the earth shall be blessed."[1]

Genesis 12:1–3 contains two great promises from God to Abraham. The first "I will" statement speaks of act one in God's redemptive program. As we read the Old Testament, we see God's "progress of redemption" occur. He will make a great nation from Abraham and does build a redemptive channel through the nation of Israel—he keeps his promise to Abraham. The second promise is that "in you all the families of the earth shall be blessed." This promise parallels Christ's statement to his twelve disciples, ". . . on this rock I will build my church, and the gates of hell shall not prevail against it." The seed promise to Abraham grows through the twelve tribes of Israel, Abraham's grandson. The seed promise of Christ will grow through

---

1. Gen 12:1–3, italics mine for emphasis.

the ministry and theology of his twelve true disciples. And just like the promise God makes to Abram, Christ will keep his promise.

ACT 2 REVIEW

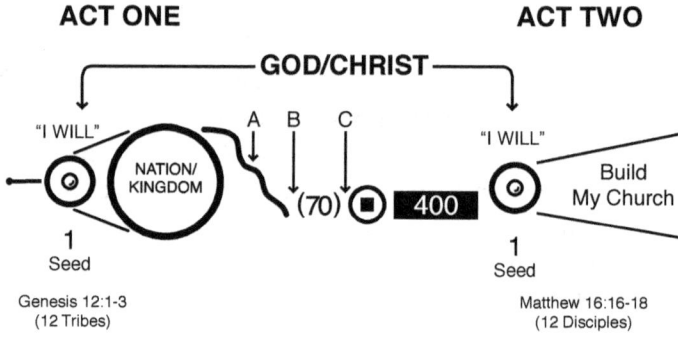

Figure One

One other parallel ought to be noted—just as a person needed to worship and sacrifice to God (Yahweh) at Jerusalem (God's designated place for getting right with him, as well as the dwelling place of his glory), so also—in act two—a person needs to become a member of the church that Christ is building in order to become right with God (through the gospel). The keys to kingdom salvation in the Old Testament (act one) are found only in joining, by faith, the community of God's people, i.e., the nation of Israel. Salvation in the Old Testament is from Yahweh and nowhere else to be found. Similarly, the keys to kingdom salvation in the new covenant (act two) are only found in the church and nowhere else. When Jesus says, "I will give you the keys of the kingdom of heaven . . ." he is indicating that those who lead his church will have the authority to open or close the door of membership to his church. God has his people, the church. And one is either inside or outside of Christ's kingdom.

The Church

In Ephesians 2:11–22, the Apostle Paul uses metaphors to help the Ephesian believers (and us) understand what the New Testament church looks like. He begins by explaining that the New Testament church, unlike the

Step One: "The Seed"

church under the old covenant (the nation of Israel) will consist of both Jews and Gentiles. In the old covenant, the Gentiles ". . . were at that time separated from Christ, alienated from the commonwealth of Israel and strangers to the covenants of promise, having no hope and without God in the world" (Eph 2:12). Gentiles, as people who lived outside of God's covenant people, were "far off" from the living God. Now, however, due to the gospel and the joining together of Gentiles and Jews, the church looks like these pictures: a new man and one body, a spiritual nation (in which they are fellow citizens), a family (one household), and a building (or structure) being constructed as a holy temple. Similarly, the Apostle Peter, describes the church of God as one flock (1 Pet 5:2).

The similarities between the Old Testament church, as expressed through the nation of Israel, and the New Testament church, made up of both Jews and Gentiles are these:

1. Both are the people of God, although the visible church in both the Old and New Testaments does not always consist of true followers of the living God. The invisible church consists of the elect of God (Rom 9:6–8; 1 John 2:19–20).

2. Both consist of many members or people. Both are known as special or treasured people, chosen by God (Deut 7:6; 1 Pet 2:9).

3. Both are united together—they find their unity in God-ordained leadership. The heads of Israel that provided their unity were Kings David and Solomon, who together pictured Christ's headship. The head of the church is Christ, the king of the universe.

4. Both are kingdoms. Israel is one nation (or kingdom) under Kings David and Solomon. The church is one spiritual kingdom serving under its king, the Lord Jesus.

However, there are also differences between the church (or people of God) as expressed in Israel and the church as expressed in one body consisting of both Jews and Gentiles. These differences are:

1. In Israel there is *one* leader (the king). In the church there are *many* leaders, i.e., elders who are appointed to each individual congregation.

2. In Israel, there was *one* channel of redemption which was *centralized*. God's presence dwelled in Jerusalem. In the church, there are *many* channels of redemption and those are *localized*, i.e., present among

the community in which they exist. God's presence is among his "gathered together" ones.

3. The nation of Israel is purely Jewish (including those from the outside who might convert to Yahweh); they are people generated from the "seed of Abraham." Israel's invitation—if one exists at all—is "come and serve Yahweh." The church is comprised of people from every tongue, tribe, and nation. It is both cosmopolitan and international in nature. The church lives under a command from its king to "go and tell the good news."

4. Israel, as an earthly nation, fought battles. Those battles were political and national in nature. The church must learn to exist in a given society. Although constantly fighting "spiritual battles," the church is non-political in its being.

5. Israel lives in the "shadows" of God's plan of redemption. God's plan is a mystery until the coming of Christ (Col 1:27; Eph 3:6). The church lives in the "full light" of Christ's coming, in accordance with the revelation of the plan of God (Rom 16:25–27).

The Book of Acts

As we follow the "birth," as well as the growing life of the early New Testament church, we must rely upon the only account provided. That account comes to us in the form of the historical record called the book of Acts. The book of Acts was written by Luke, the author of the gospel account of Christ bearing his name. Acts is considered to be the history of the church in its earliest days. Just as Luke introduces his gospel record of Christ as an account of "all that Jesus began to do and teach . . ." (Acts 1:1), so the book of Acts is an account of all that Jesus *continued* to do and teach through the ministry of Holy Spirit-led disciples. In Acts 1:8, Luke provides a second version of Jesus's "Great Commission" and in doing so, supplies a summary statement of the entire book. After his resurrection, Jesus promises that he will send the Holy Spirit to empower his followers. Luke writes Jesus's words, "But you will receive power when the Holy Spirit has come upon you, and you will be my witnesses in Jerusalem and in all Judea and Samaria, and to the end of the earth." Luke's book will be broken down into these three categories:

Step One: "The Seed"

1. To Jerusalem (Acts 1–7)
2. To Judea and Samaria (Acts 8–11:18)
3. To the ends of the earth (Acts 11:19–28:31)

After giving these assuring and promising words, Jesus visibly and bodily ascends into heaven (through the heavens), alongside—as Luke records it—an angelic promise that he will return in similar fashion.

When the disciples are gathered at Pentecost, the falling of the Holy Spirit, along with his power, is recounted in Acts chapter 2. The Spirit becomes the very heart and life of the church. As a prelude of things to come, Jews from many nations hear God glorified in their own dialects, through the medium of miraculous tongues spoken in their native languages. These recipients subsequently hear the gospel message of the crucified and resurrected Christ from the lips of Peter.

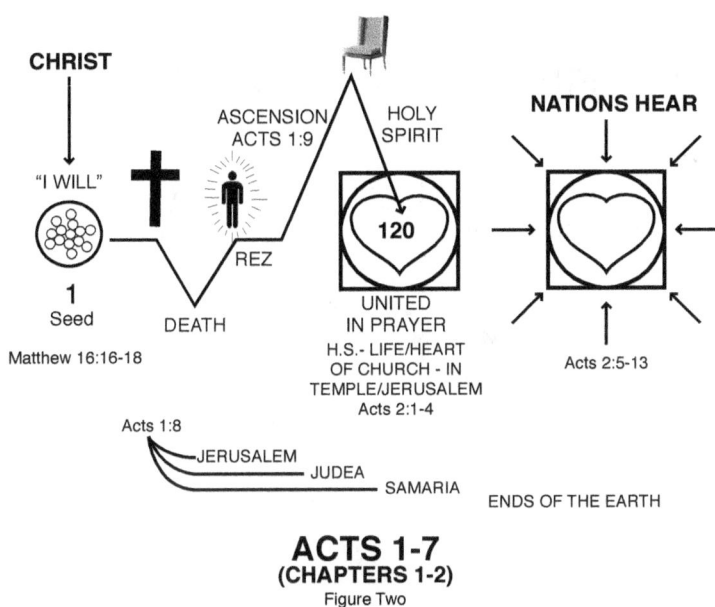

ACT 2
STEP ONE: THE SEED GROWS

ACTS 1-7
(CHAPTERS 1-2)
Figure Two

After Peter's persuasive sermon of explanation, approximately three thousand listeners are converted to Christ. As described in Acts 2:42–47, this newly formed church (which is not yet the cosmopolitan church it will become) is typified by the following attributes:

1. The Apostles' teaching
2. Fellowship
3. The sacraments (breaking of bread)
4. Prayer
5. A sense of awe
6. Apostolic miracles
7. Unity and community
8. Mercy (sharing with those in need)
9. Meals together and open homes (hospitality)
10. Praise and gladness
11. The favor of the people (the masses)
12. Evangelistic growth

The church remains in the temple during these formative days.

ACT 2
STEP ONE: THE SEED GROWS

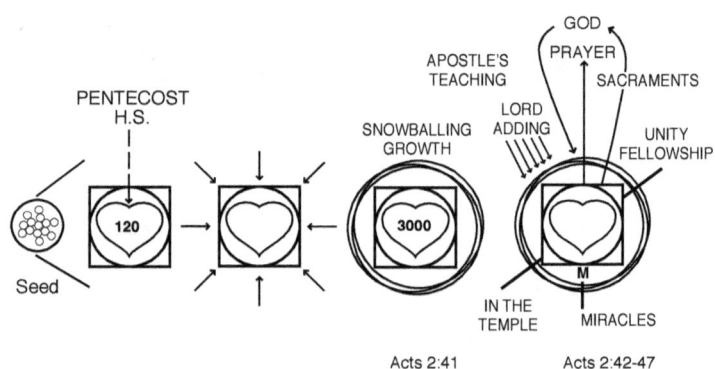

ACTS 1-7
(CHAPTER 2)
Figure Three

Step One: "The Seed"

Step One: The Seed Grows

The seed of the church consists of the disciples who adhere to Peter's confession, "You are the Christ, the Son of the living God." The life of the church will sprout from this seed, i.e., the twelve who believe this confession. Peter's insightful declaration represents the beliefs of Jesus's disciples and encapsulates the life-giving truth of the gospel to be proclaimed to all. The doctrine of Christ's deity provides the necessary doctrinal substance that brings vast potential to the future of the church. Upon that truth, Christ will build his church. This confession will bring about a proliferation of Christ-followers who will flourish, despite certain opposition, in the context of the world's soil.

The seed of the church will germinate at Pentecost (the falling of the Holy Spirit among the waiting disciples). The seed promise of Christ, "I will build my church" will come to fruition through the power of the Holy Spirit. The seed will be conceived in the womb of a nation—the nation of Israel. This seed will start in Jerusalem and, of all places, at the temple ("the house" mentioned in Acts 2:2 is implied as being the temple precincts).[2] In Acts 2:46, after the experience of Pentecost, including the conversion of approximately three thousand people, we read, "And day by day, attending the temple together and breaking bread in their homes, they received their food with glad and generous hearts . . ." Even after the great spiritual explosion of Pentecost, the expanded followers *remain* in the temple area. They are not yet "the church," but a sect of people associated with the temple. In Acts 3:1, we read a dynamic story about the healing of a lame man by Peter, the great Pentecostal preacher—yet, these new converts continue in the confines of the temple of Israel. This growing band of believers, and their leaders, appears to be fixated on the temple locale and the life they have discovered in a temple-oriented community of faith.

However, the seed has certainly grown. It has surged from one hundred and twenty believers in Acts 1:15 to around three thousand by Acts 2:41.[3] It then grows to over five thousand followers, as recorded in Acts 2:47 (continued growth) and in Acts 4:4.[4] Suddenly, reminiscent of Israel's growth in Egypt (as recorded in Exodus 1:5), Jerusalem appears "filled" with Christ-followers! And although still tethered to the temple, this bur-

---

2. Bruce, *Book of Acts*, 55.
3. Due to the Pentecostal outpouring of the Holy Spirit.
4. The men alone made up this number.

geoning group is beginning to invade temple space and gain much notice. What is their doctrine? Simply this: Jesus died and was raised from the dead. Are they primarily a mass of disorganized novice converts to Christ? They are not. By Acts chapter 6, they tackle an internal dispute and quickly distinguish between those who teach and those who serve. This group of believers is becoming organized, and subsequently move to select what are essentially the first deacons (servants) to meet the growing needs of their people.

They have become a group (a church) within a group (a nation). Like the enslaved Israelites in Egypt, who were "a nation within a nation," this new and multiplying band of believers needs to get "out" of their potentially unfavorable circumstances. They now have unity, organization, presence, solidarity, and vibrant life. Additionally, their growth is surely adding an air of excitement to their movement, as well as possible persecution by the establishment. However, we must note that they are not yet a church. They remain:

1. In a central location
2. Small—only one in number (although admittedly quite large as a group—today, we would call them a megachurch)
3. Only Jewish in composition—not yet international

Opposition and Persecution

Step one is defined as a fledgling church existing within the confines or the circumference of the Jerusalem temple. It encompasses chapters 1–7 of Acts. In order for the church to become *the church* (consisting of both Jews and Gentiles), a number of contributing factors must occur. Unfortunately, this means that both opposition and persecution are necessary. We will see these agents of change occur in the chapters leading up to the church's dispersion among the "peoples" of the world as recorded in Acts chapter 8. Opposition might be defined as mild interference and outside pressure to conform to local and cultural expectations. Persecution might be defined as opposition taken to the next level, and includes the threat of death for those who express and maintain their commitment to Christ and his mission, and also actual death, as seen in the stoning of the church's first martyr.

Step One: "The Seed"

Persecution 1: Opposition

Luke follows up the fabulous results of the Pentecostal moment in Acts chapter 2 with the account of one of many miracles performed by the apostles. This miracle involves the healing of a man who was lame for over forty years (Acts 4:22). Acts chapter 3 is the record of this healing. In this chapter, Luke continues to write about the ensuing confrontation that such a public and significant miracle causes in the presence of the religious leaders—the priests, the captain of the temple guard, and the Sadducees (who did not like the proclamation of the resurrection from the dead). Luke summarizes the result, "And they arrested them and put them in custody until the next day, for it was already evening" (Acts 4:3). This arrest is what I call "opposition," and in this case, I will call it "Persecution 1." Not only is it relatively mild, but it is also beneficial to the cause of the gospel. Luke clearly makes the point that ". . . many of those who had heard the word believed, and the number of the men came to about five thousand" (Acts 4:4).

So, in the case of Persecution 1 (opposition), we see the following results, each of which are quite positive:

1. Many believe and the church grows to over five thousand men (4:4).
2. The disciples, especially Peter, grow in their boldness in proclaiming Christ's crucifixion and resurrection (4:8–10). They remain committed to their Lord and their mission to proclaim him.
3. They are strengthened as a praying church (4:24–30).
4. They are filled in a greater way with the Holy Spirit and with further boldness (4:31).
5. They exhibit increased unity ("one heart and soul"—4:32) and continue to share possessions with one another in a communal fashion (4:32, 34–37).
6. Their witness to Christ and his resurrection increases in greater power (4:33).

As we read chapter 4 in Luke's account of the acts of the apostles, we would certainly conclude that opposition (or Persecution 1) has not caused the church to lose hope or momentum; it is still growing and stable.

Pollution

In Acts chapter 5, we see a shift in the perils of the church. The young Christian community, still meeting in Jerusalem, has not only survived the problem of outward opposition, but conversely has thrived in the face of such mistreatment. But what will happen to them if the inevitable problem of *inward* trials takes place? Such a trial will be seen in the case of a deceptively greedy married couple as told in Acts chapter 5. I will call this event the testing of internal "pollution" that threatens the church.

In a very vivid story line, Luke illustrates the peril of lying to God, the Holy Spirit. The married couple, Ananias and Sapphira, are purged from the church in miraculous fashion—both die immediately upon detection—in order to demonstrate that those inside the church must be sincere and genuine, even in the seemingly noblest of actions. God desires a pure church and will effectively remove those impediments that threaten the vessel which radiates the wonderful proclamation of his son. He will not allow this pollution to become part of the early church culture. The consequences of this "cleansing" of false professors of faith is made clear: "great fear came upon the whole church and upon all who heard of these things" (Acts 5:11). Onlookers in the temple area now watch the apostolic miracles with greater respect and higher esteem, although they are wary of joining a community of such austere power. Nevertheless, Luke tells us, "And more than ever believers were added to the Lord, multitudes of both men and women . . ." (Acts 5:14). The church continues to grow. And these believers—both sexes—have apparently experienced true and genuine conversions in light of the recent process of purging false professors.

Persecution 2: Testing

The account of the second stage of persecution of the church I will label as testing. This stage is called thusly on the basis that to go through opposition *twice* is a true testing of the faith, life, and perseverance of the church. This second incident of persecution, recounted in Acts 5:17–41, is also truly described as a testing of faith in that the apostles almost meet death (5:33). Ultimately, they are only flogged (presumably whipped with thirty-nine lashes). However, the end result of this grand test of faith is, that although beaten and charged to speak no further in the name of Jesus, "they left the presence of the council, rejoicing that they were counted worthy to

Step One: "The Seed"

suffer dishonor for the name. And every day in the temple, and from house to house, they did not cease teaching and preaching that the Christ is Jesus" (Acts 5:41–41). These apostles have been tested, and not only rejoiced in their trial, but remained undeterred in their mission. Jesus continued to be preached, both in the temple arena and from house to house. Luke assures the reader that the number of the disciples continued to increase despite their obstacles (Acts 6:1a).

ACT 2
STEP ONE: THE SEED GROWS
OPPOSITION/PERSECUTION/GROWTH

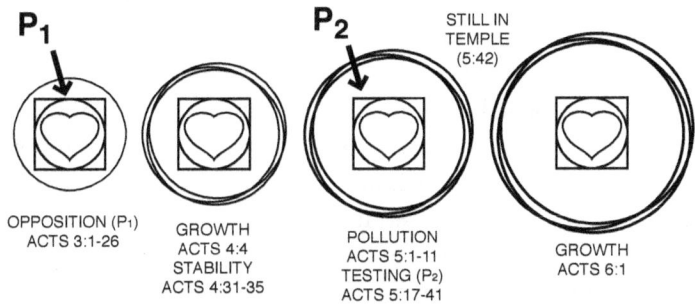

ACTS 1-7
(3:1-6:1)
Figure Four

Persecution 3: To the Death

As the church continues to thrive and grow, a problem arises in the communal/sharing practices evident in these early days (Acts 6:1–6). The Hellenistic (Greek) Jews raise a complaint against the native Jews (Hebrews) because their widows are being overlooked in the daily rationing of food for the meals. Problem solving is posited and the solution (choosing deacon-like individuals of high reputation and Greek names—and thus probably Greek origins—to serve)[5] brings to the forefront two individuals (among

---

5. Bruce, *Book of Acts*, 129.

seven) who are crucial to the narrative that Luke is recording: Stephen and Philip. These two servants/deacons would naturally be less temple-fixated than the Aramaic speaking Jews and are therefore primed to help lead the break of the church (still fully Jewish) from its orientation toward the temple.

According to Acts chapter 6, verse 7, the following positive attributes of the church are sustained, "And the word of God continued to increase, and the number of the disciples multiplied greatly in Jerusalem, and a great many of the priests became obedient to the faith." In this short verse, however, Luke notes one major element that is going to cause even greater persecution for the church: the mention of "priests." It is one thing for the masses to follow the leadership of these surprisingly capable, enthusiastic, bold, and brave disciples of Jesus; it is quite another for Israel's own spiritual leaders—the priests—to listen to the preaching and "cave into" this novel message. And it is not simply a priest or two. Luke says "many priests" were becoming obedient to the faith. Surely, they were believing in the crucified and resurrected messiah and joining the highly conspicuous activities of this growing Jerusalem congregation. Praying, sharing, praising, fellowshipping, receiving the sacraments, listening, and believing. Losing priests to this new movement would certainly irritate and incense the local Jewish leaders.

The testimony of Stephen's powerful ministry brings this situation to a head. His spirit of grace, power, and ability to perform miracles and wonders arouses a variety of men from the synagogue to take him on in debate. They are no match for Stephen, so they secretly instigate other men to maliciously slander him. They stir up the masses and religious leaders to drag him away to trial before the Sanhedrin (the Jewish supreme council). False witnesses come forward to accuse Stephen. The two false accusations against him that probably include a minimum of truth, are:

1. He is against Moses and therefore he is against God (Acts 6:11)
2. He is against the temple (Acts 6: 13–14)

In response to these phony charges, Stephen commences preaching a sermon that covers "God's Progress of Redemption" throughout the Old Testament, up through the glorious kingdom of David and Solomon. He addresses their accusations and preaches two prevailing themes:

Step One: "The Seed"

1. The Jews have constantly rejected God's message and messengers. They have always rebelled against God's purposes, including Moses himself (Acts 7:25, 35, 39, 41–43, 51–53)
2. God does not necessarily dwell in the temple (Acts 7:2, 20, 30, 33, 44, 47–50)

In a move that would make any modern day evangelist shudder, Stephen presents his "altar call" in Acts 7:51–53,

> 51 You stiff-necked people, uncircumcised in heart and ears, you always resist the Holy Spirit. As your fathers did, so do you. 52 Which of the prophets did your fathers not persecute? And they killed those who announced beforehand the coming of the Righteous One, whom you have now betrayed and murdered, 53 you who received the law as delivered by angels and did not keep it.

According to Acts 7:57, after having become enraged and grinded their teeth toward him, and having cried out in a loud voice with covered ears, they do indeed come forward in response to his altar call—but to attack him. Luke recounts that he is full of the Holy Spirit, and sees the glory of God, as well as Jesus standing at the right hand of God; as he declares what he sees, they drive him out of the city and stone him to death. Stephen becomes the first Christian martyr and his death is another in the aforementioned series of Israel's rejection of God's messengers. However, Luke adds a very important note that will grow into major significance later,

> 58 And the witnesses laid down their garments at the feet of a young man named *Saul*. 59 And as they were stoning Stephen, he called out, "Lord Jesus, receive my spirit." 60 And falling to his knees he cried out with a loud voice, "Lord, do not hold this sin against them." And when he had said this, he fell asleep.[6]

Saul apparently sees Stephen's death and willing martyrdom for Christ, and hears his cry to Jesus[7] as well as his words of forgiveness toward his murderers. Surely, the future apostle is intrigued at this event and would remember it vividly (we can presume that he probably told Luke about it on one of their missionary journeys together).

---

6. Acts 7:58b–59; italics mine for emphasis.
7. F. F. Bruce suggests that Stephen's cry to Jesus is an early, if tacit, testimony to the Christian belief in our Lord's essential deity, 171.

So Send I You

The prospect of full scale persecution, with its daunting foreshadowing of possible death, has led the reader to the end of step one. This organically growing congregation consisting of thousands of Jewish believers in Christ has yielded at least the primary step of Christ's "seed promise" to Peter and his fellow disciples: "I will build my church . . ." The first portion of the Great Commission given in Acts 1:8 has been realized. "But you will receive power when the Holy Spirit has come upon you, and you will be my witnesses in Jerusalem . . ." The seed promise has grown quickly, and Christ's Holy Spirit has provided both the power and the increase of the church. Step one, however, has seen the church remain in Jerusalem, with an orientation toward the temple. It cannot remain there forever, as idyllic as the setting might seem to these "love struck by Jesus" believers. We need to continue to step two in the church's journey.

ACT TWO
STEP ONE: THE SEED GROWS
PERSECUTION TO DEATH

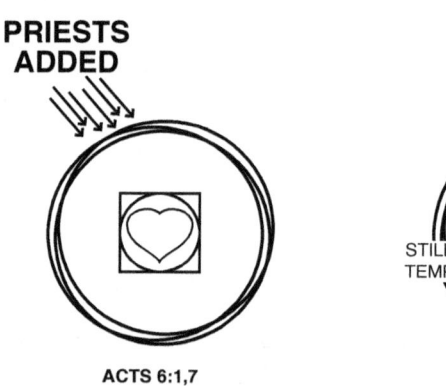
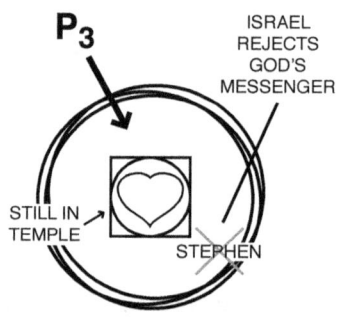

ACTS 1-7
(6:1-7:60)
Figure Five

Step Two: "Out" of Jerusalem

Persecution 4: Full-force and Officially Sanctioned

ACTS CHAPTER 7 IS as long as it is strategic in making its point about the heightening Jewish persecution of the church. Stephen's sermon is an expansion of the many confrontations that Jesus had had with the Jewish religious leaders of his day, and in some ways, more provocative. His death led to an inevitable conclusion, as addressed by Luke. Persecution of the church is now "true" persecution, i.e., officially sanctioned and legally approved, as demonstrated by Saul's own approval of Stephen's demise at the hands of stone throwers.

Saul's presence at Stephen's martyrdom is significant, and worse yet, his approval of his execution spawns the following repercussions (both negative and yet serendipitously positive) as stated by Luke, "And there arose on that day a great persecution against the church in Jerusalem, and they were all scattered throughout the regions of Judea and Samaria, except the apostles" (Acts 8:1). Now, full-forced and officially sanctioned persecution of the worse type breaks out against the church. Believers' lives are endangered, and Jerusalem is the obvious and immediate target since it is the center for this new Jewish "cult."

However, there is one incredible benefit to this large scale persecution. Although Jerusalem, and in essence the nation of Israel, are now rejected as primary recipients of the gospel (Israelite leaders having driven out this massive congregation of Jewish Christians), the gospel is now making waves in the surrounding domains. Christ is being taken to Judea and Samaria! And it is not even the apostles who are spreading the message. Believers from all over the surrounding territories, who had gathered in Jerusalem for the celebration of the Passover, are now scattered all around. Jesus's Great Commission, as expressed by Luke in Acts 1:8, is finally coming to fruition. In Acts 8:2 we see that the nature of the redemptive channel is no longer confined to southern Israel and Jerusalem (and the temple), but has also been dispersed among the peoples of Judah.

Who would covet persecution for their cause? We see the threat of severe persecution and probable loss of life drive believers (or church laypersons) either to return home, or to flee from the focal persecution. Waiting in the wings, ready to take center stage, is the primary activist in the church's persecution, the man named Saul. Luke writes, "But Saul was ravaging the church, and entering house after house, he dragged off men and women and committed them to prison" (Acts 8:3). Luke briefly diverts the reader away from the fleeing mass of believers and their newfound faith in order to portray their source of greatest persecution, Saul. Luke teases us with this mention of a frenzied man who is filled with resentment and deep hatred for these blasphemous zealots for Jesus. But Luke is providing this glimpse of Saul in order to demonstrate the glory of God's grace and his converting power.

No worries, however, according to Luke. Although Saul is lurking in the dark in order to find and imprison followers of Jesus, Luke points out the very same observation that he makes in Act 8:1. In Acts 8:4 he states the general principle that emanates from these believers who are scattered by the upscale efforts of persecution toward them, "Now those who were scattered went about preaching the word." The word of God is being hailed and proclaimed everywhere these disbanded and distributed laypeople go. The "footnote" about the ravages of Saul upon God's people is sandwiched between two glorious verses declaring the victory of the word as it pushes its way well outside of the Jerusalem setting in which it first took root.

And then there is Samaria. Luke has told his readers that the persecution has scattered believers throughout both Judea and Samaria. Samaria was not a popular area to the Jews. Those living there were of a mixed national race. They were looked down upon by the Jews because of their Jewish-Gentile heritage. In the eyes of the Jews this made them lesser, second class citizens. They were also considered to be a religiously mixed race, making their worship an inferior product in contrast to the purity of Jerusalem's religious practices. Victory (gospel proclamation) is followed by apparent defeat (persecution leading to the death of Stephen), but the good news of Jesus is creeping into unexplored territory. The Samaritans will hear!

Luke tells us in Acts 8:5 that Philip travels to the city of Samaria (we are not certain which city this might be) where he proclaims Christ to its

Step Two: "Out" of Jerusalem

people. Philip's boldness of stepping into "foreign" territory with the gospel is rewarded by God. His Samaritan listeners are prepared and receptive, giving him their attention. Miraculous works attend his preaching, and people are healed of unclean spirits, paralysis, and lameness. The city is filled with gospel joy! Luke writes, "But when they believed Philip as he preached good news about the kingdom of God and the name of Jesus Christ, they were baptized, both men and women" (Acts 8: 12). Most significantly, however, is that once the apostles in Jerusalem hear that the Samaritans are receiving the word of God, Peter and John are sent and the Samaritans receive the Holy Spirit through Peter's apostolic authority (Acts 8:14–17).

The falling of the Holy Spirit upon the Samaritans occurs through the laying on of hands by the apostles, and although tongues are not mentioned, the obvious power is such that an onlooker, Simon, a former magician, wants this special ability. The point of the narrative, however, is that a two-fold assurance is provided with regard to the movement of the church outside of Jerusalem:

1. Receiving the Holy Spirit assures the Samaritans that they are fully incorporated into the newly founded community of believers.[1]

2. The reception of the Holy Spirit by the Samaritans assures the Jews (particularly these Jewish Christians) that God has given these previously despised and hated Samaritan neighbors the blessing of the indwelling Spirit. The Jewish Christians can now recognize that the giving of the Holy Spirit is intended to be a universal blessing.

In Acts 8:25, we read a beautiful summary statement of what has happened in the lives and hearts of both Peter and John as they return home to Jerusalem, "Now when they had testified and spoken the word of the Lord, they returned to Jerusalem, preaching the gospel to many villages of the Samaritans." They have caught the vision—God loves the Samaritans! These two prominent apostles return to Jerusalem functioning like Methodist itinerate circuit riding preachers, stopping and proclaiming the gospel to any Samaritan who will listen. Luke's commentary in chapter 8 signifies the reality that the gospel has moved out of Jerusalem, starting with Samaria (8:1, 5, 14, 25).

---

1. Additionally, the original disciples were Jewish when they received the Holy Spirit at Pentecost. Yet now the formally outcast Samaritans had similarly received the Holy Spirit, confirming their entrance into the body of Christ.

Luke then provides us with a hint of what is to come—the gospel will surely advance to that even greater and unexpected region—the world of the Gentiles. Philip, an early leader of the Hellenistic sub-group of the early church in Jerusalem, is apparently ever the evangelist with a vision for those on the "outside." On the way to Gaza, travelling on a desert road, Philip providentially runs into an Ethiopian man sitting in his chariot on his return from a visit to Jerusalem. And what was this Ethiopian doing as he sat? Reading the Bible (technically, the Old Testament). Upon first glance, Philip, as a Jewish convert to Christ, might conclude that the Ethiopian is no candidate for Christianity. This stranger is a Gentile, a black African, and a eunuch reading an obscure (to him) text from the prophet Isaiah. Yet, through Philip's willingness and effort, we see the gospel leaping over significant barriers in this single encounter—and a wonderful thing occurs. The Ethiopian traveler believes the gospel, is baptized in some apparently rare pool of water, and then suddenly Philip is gone, whisked away by the Spirit. The evangelist is found in Azotus (modern day Ashdod) near the coast and then travels up the coastline preaching the gospel until he reaches Caesarea. There, he apparently settles down, raises a family and possibly becomes a local evangelist or pastor (Acts 21:8). The gospel is certainly spreading in many regions.

Review

Step one described the Pentecostal explosion of the Holy Spirit that reverberated throughout Jerusalem as the New Testament church was born in the cradle of the temple. This church is wholly Jewish and lingers in Jerusalem as it seems to grow exponentially in relationship to the resistance, opposition, and persecution poured out upon it. The positives outweigh the negatives, but the wonderful qualities of this new Christian fellowship are dampened by the reality that the church has become comfortable in its home environment. The church remains one; she needs to become many. The church thrives in one location; however, she needs to spread to other communities. She is Jewish in her origin, but needs to go out into the world.

However, in step two, we see that the ultimate result of pervasive and harrowing persecution disperses the redemptive channel as God's people begin to take the gospel to Judea and Samaria. The church is growing, but is not yet mature. In John 4:23, Jesus tells the woman at the well—the Samaritan woman—these words, "But the hour is coming, and is now here,

Step Two: "Out" of Jerusalem

when the true worshipers will worship the Father in spirit and truth, for the Father is seeking such people to worship him." Indeed, the hour is coming when others outside of Jerusalem are going to gain the great privilege of hearing the gospel, learning of the crucified and resurrected Lord and Savior, Jesus Christ.

While recognizing the vast progress the gospel has made when moving from step one[2] to step two—the gospel to Judea and Samaria—we are faced with a question at the end of Acts 8: "Are we ready to go to the Gentiles?" We are almost ready for this big leap of gospel inclusion; however, two things need to happen.

1. We need a special messenger to go to the Gentiles. In amazing fashion, he is secured for the work, as seen in the account of Acts chapter 9.
2. We need to break down an old and major barrier that could prevent full acceptance of Gentile believers. This is accomplished by extraordinary means in the account written by Luke in Acts 9:32–11:18.

In Acts chapters 8–11, we have the accounts of three major individuals involved in the transition of Jewish Christianity to a mature Christian church—one that includes Gentiles. We have already observed Philip's role in Acts chapter 8. The other two individuals are the Apostles Paul and Peter.[3] They are presented in this historic narrative in alphabetical order (there is nothing "inspired" about that, but it can help the reader to remember the transition from step two to step three).

---

2. A temple-oriented Jewish church meeting in Jerusalem.

3. I summarize these three individuals using a mnemonic device: PH-PL-PT (pronounced *Fuh*, *Pluh*, and *Petuh*).

ACT TWO
STEP TWO
"OUT" OF JERUSALEM

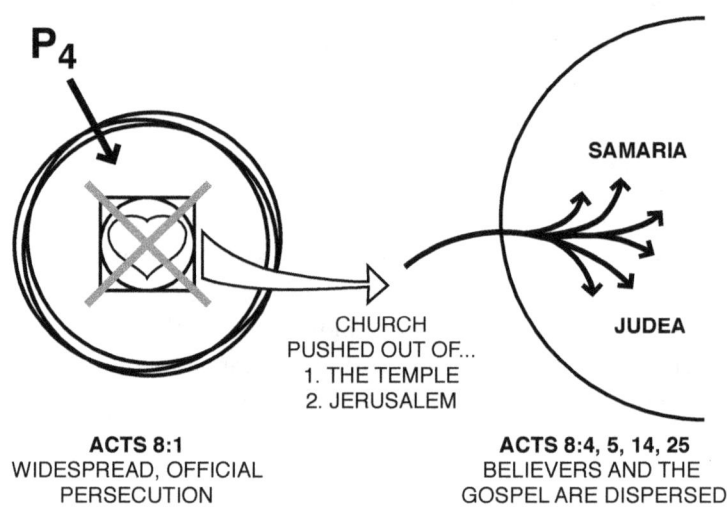

ACTS 8:1-25
Figure Six

Step Three: "To The Gentiles"

THE CHURCH NEEDS TO move forward with becoming universal for all people and all nations. Luke begins Acts chapter 9 with a picture of Saul, the growing church's zealous nemesis that won't go away. Last seen in Acts 7:58, and in 8:1 and 3, he has been persecuting the church in Jerusalem. In Acts chapter 9 he is willing to threaten and even murder Christ-followers anywhere he can find them. He plans to go to Damascus in order to gain letters granting him the authority to "arrest" and bind anyone belonging to "the way" in order to bring them to Jerusalem. We must give him some Pharisaical credit for following the law and not "asking for forgiveness rather than permission"—though apparently he does gain permission from the high priest to go to the synagogues at Damascus. His would be a short journey with a new destination, a trip which involves quite the surprise.

We might ask, "Why Saul/Paul?" As we shall soon discover, Peter is simply too Jewish, too locally minded, and too uneducated in Gentile thought and lifestyle. I believe that there are at least three answers for why God chose Paul (PL) to take his message to the Gentiles:

1. He has the proper religious background—he believes in the one true God of the Scriptures (Acts 22:3).

2. He has the proper cultural and intellectual background. He is born and raised in Tarsus, the university city of the Roman Empire (Acts 22:3), and has studied under the honorable scholar, Gamaliel (Acts 5:34; Acts 22:3). Saul knows both the Jewish and Gentile worlds.

3. As a Roman citizen, he has the proper political background (Acts 16:37).

Saul is our man, but there is a problem: he is moving in the wrong direction with a fury and needs to be turned around; he needs to be converted. In Luke's account, that is exactly what happens. In Acts 9:1–19, Saul is dramatically converted to the resurrected Christ. According to Luke, he goes almost immediately from breathing threats toward believers in Christ to proclaiming Jesus, saying, "He is the Son of God" (Acts 9:20). He has gone from persecuting to preaching—quite the conversion. God has been looking for someone to take the church to the next level, someone who will provide the leadership and the expertise (submitted to the Holy Spirit) needed to make the ministry and the focus of the church international. Luke explains God's choice in this manner, through the words of Ananias, as he quotes God's message to him, "Go, for he is a chosen instrument of mine to carry my name before the Gentiles and kings and the children of Israel" (Acts 9:15). Paul's ministry will be an international one! He will be the apostle to the Gentiles, and thus to "everybody." To prove how serious Paul's reversal in passion has become, Luke points out that this new convert soon begins to speak and argue with the same Hellenistic Jews who stoned Stephen (remember, he was there watching and approving this murder).[1] They attempt to murder Paul as well, until he is transported away to Caesarea and then to Tarsus, temporarily removing him from controversy.

At this point in the narrative, Luke throws in another of his patented and positive summaries about the growth and state of the diversifying church, "So the church throughout all Judea and Galilee and Samaria had peace and was being built up. And walking in the fear of the Lord and in the comfort of the Holy Spirit, it multiplied" (Acts 9:31). Pitted against their greatest human foe, God has not only expanded and sanctified the church through the Holy Spirit, he has transformed her primary antagonist. The church's chief persecutor is now alive in Christ. In a few years, he will write about the impact of his conversion with these words, "I have been crucified with Christ. It is no longer I who live, but Christ who lives in me. And the life I now live in the flesh I live by faith in the Son of God, who loved me and gave himself for me" (Gal 2:20). Because of his conversion, the church is now enjoying a peace devoid of persecution and thus, it continues to grow.

We return to the question, "Are we ready to go to the Gentiles?" Asking that question actually leads us to three other questions:

1. What will the reaction be should God thrust the gospel message immediately and directly to the "despised" Gentiles with ensuing conversions as a result?

---

1. Bruce, *Book of Acts*, 207.

Step Three: "To The Gentiles"

2. What will the Jewish Christians say about (and how would they respond to) those converted Gentiles?
3. What will the apostles say about those converted Gentiles?

Acts 9:31 has made it very clear that the church has flourished in Jerusalem (unmentioned, but assumed), Judea, and Samaria. What could hinder its advancement into the Gentile world? The answer is inexplicable: a subsequent controversy between Jew and Gentile could easily brew into a considerable schism in the life of the church. In this regard, one major stumbling block remains and must be removed in order to effectively proclaim the gospel to the Gentiles. That issue will be addressed under the acrostic "PT," and is another factor in the completion of step three.

Beginning in Acts chapter 9 (verse 32), Peter (*Petuh*) returns to the forefront of Luke's narrative. The text tells us that he travels to the coastal city of Joppa after hearing about the death of a woman named Dorcas. Through Peter's ministry, Dorcas is raised from the dead. This miracle grants Peter an increasing opportunity to declare the gospel and many unbelievers come to the Lord. Peter remains in Joppa, and in God's providence, it becomes a place that will help prepare him to sympathize with the forthcoming gospel proclamation to the Gentiles. Luke writes, "And he stayed in Joppa for many days with one Simon, a tanner" (Acts 9:43).

Simon, the tanner, lives on the Mediterranean Sea (Acts 10:6). Staying on the beachfront for some time, we could surmise that Peter looks across the ocean horizon, and with transcendent reflection, thinks about the needs of the world. Surely, *they* need to hear the gospel. Staying with Simon the tanner is also unusual because tanning deals with dead animals, making it an "unclean" occupation for the Jews.[2] Once again considering Peter's lodgings—amongst dead animals on an ocean shore—we are left to wonder if his sensitivity to some of the Jewish ceremonial laws and traditions might be breaking down.[3]

Peter is presently in Joppa, but Luke shifts the scene to a man named Cornelius in Caesarea. He is a Roman centurion (clearly a Gentile) who is also known as a "God fearer."[4] Nevertheless he is a Gentile. Cornelius is

---

2. "And if any animal which you may eat dies, whoever touches its carcass shall be unclean until the evening, and whoever eats of its carcass shall wash his clothes and be unclean until the evening. And whoever carries the carcass shall wash his clothes and be unclean until the evening..." Lev 11:39–40.

3. Bruce, *Book of Acts*, 213.

4. Meaning that he believed in Yahweh but was not in a relationship with him;

not a likely candidate for Peter's evangelism. However, through a vision, Cornelius sees an angel who calls his name, tells him that his prayers to God have been heard, and that he must send men to Joppa to retrieve Peter. Interestingly, he sends three men, two servants and a devout soldier, to Joppa. We might wonder, "why doesn't God send Cornelius *to Philip* who has settled in Caesarea (Acts 8:40) and who is a proven and capable evangelist?" The answer must be that Peter needs to be convinced that Gentiles are to become a part of the church. It is apparent, by observing Philip's previous evangelistic efforts, that he needs no convincing. However, as for Peter, God must break down any prejudicial barriers that might surface due to his inherent Jewishness. We might also wonder, "Why doesn't God simply send Cornelius to Peter, where he is residing in Joppa?" Or, "Why doesn't God simply explain the gospel to Cornelius using an angel?" The likely answer is that Peter must "Go!" He must fulfill Christ's Great Commission (Matt 28:18–20). God is making a powerful point—Peter must realize that Gentiles, as a group, are not "unclean." He must observe, not one God-fearing Gentile, but *many* Gentiles entering into the kingdom concurrently. A secondary purpose of Peter's journey is that the effort involved in taking the trip will allow time for a group to be recruited and to congregate at Cornelius's home.

In the meantime, God is indeed at work. As Peter prays on the housetop (note that particular location for one's "personal devotional life") just before meal time, he falls into a trance. He experiences a vision of unclean animals being lowered from heaven on a sheet. A voice tells him to kill and eat. He balks at this strange command. However, the vision and command to eat occurs three times. After the sheet holding the unclean animals is taken away into the sky, it is as if Peter hears a knock on the door (the three "Gentile" men from Cornelius arrive at the gate of the house). The message on the roof has come to the gate of the house. The number "three" is not too difficult for Peter to discern.

I should mention that when I first met my future wife in the fall of 1977, I almost immediately asked her out for a date.[5] She turned me down. I asked again. She turned me down again. Eventually, I asked her out for the entire University of South Carolina Gamecock football season that fall but she was already booked—for the entire season. Understandably, I gave up trying. Time passed—over a year went by. Then she and her best friend vis-

---

nevertheless, he honored God and prayed to him.

5. I was introduced to her by a son of James "Buck" Hatch.

Step Three: "To the Gentiles"

ited a small church one Sunday morning where I was assisting the pastor as a seminary intern. I gave the children's sermon during the worship service and my wife told her friend, "He asked me out a long time ago." She replied, "You should follow up on that." As my wife left the service, the pastor and I stood at the front door greeting the departing worshipers. My future wife stopped and said, "I'm going out of town to Florida but I'll be back in three weeks—three weeks. I'll be here in three weeks." Guess what? I got the message. Three weeks passed, I saw her at her home church[6] that Sunday evening, asked her out, and almost overnight, we were on our first real date eating at LaBrasca's Pizza in Columbia, South Carolina. Within two months we were engaged (though it has worked out, do not try that method). *Three weeks* mentioned three times in what was about three seconds! How could I miss it?

Luke writes:

> 19 And while Peter was pondering the vision, the Spirit said to him, "Behold, three men are looking for you. 20 Rise and go down and accompany them without hesitation, for I have sent them." 21 And Peter went down to the men and said, "I am the one you are looking for. What is the reason for your coming?" 22 And they said, "Cornelius, a centurion, an upright and God-fearing man, who is well spoken of by the whole Jewish nation, was directed by a holy angel to send for you to come to his house and to hear what you have to say." 23 So he invited them in to be his guests.[7]

Peter readily welcomes the three Gentile messengers. Their arrival makes the vision and its message very clear, "What God has made clean, do not call common" (Acts 10:15). Peter goes with Cornelius's men and when he arrives, Cornelius has gathered quite the Gentile crowd—in his home are both relatives and close friends, a crowd assembled and ready to hear Peter's message. Peter and Cornelius share their mutual visions with each other, and it is clear that Peter is to preach the gospel to this assembled group of anticipating listeners. Luke states, "And he said to them, 'You yourselves know how unlawful it is for a Jew to associate with or to visit anyone of another nation, but God has shown me that I should not call any person common or unclean'" (Acts 10:28). As God's chosen and "set apart" people, God had forbidden the Jews from associating with those who were not. This practice was not one based on prejudice (though some Jews would

---

6. Where she was a youth director.
7. Acts 10:19–23.

certainly use that assumption at times to create a spirit of bias and superiority), but was founded upon the Israelite "law of separation (or holiness)" (Lev 19:1–2, ff., Ezra 9:1). God has shown Peter that this law is no longer to be applied by the Jews. He is to realize that although God was originally partial to the Jews as his chosen people, he no longer shows that partiality.

Thus, Peter begins his sermon with these words, "Truly I understand that God shows no partiality, 35 but in *every nation* anyone who fears him and does what is right is acceptable to him" (Acts 10:34–35). He ends with these words, "To him all the prophets bear witness that *everyone* who believes in him receives forgiveness of sins through his name" (Acts 10:43).[8] Peter doesn't even give an altar call or an invitation to believe. The Holy Spirit falls upon the people while they are listening, leaving Peter's companions amazed because the recipients of the Holy Spirit are Gentiles. Like the Pentecostal outpouring, and the Samaritan pouring out of the Holy Spirit, these Gentiles are speaking in tongues and exalting God. They are then baptized in the name of Jesus Christ. This event is a *radical change* in God's perceived plan of redemption. Someone can meet and know God without becoming a Jew! This is incredible progress, a move forward which was previously unrealized.[9]

In regard to this monumental event, Luke writes, "Now the apostles and the brothers who were throughout Judea heard that the Gentiles also had received the word of God" (Acts 11:1). But when this stunning news reaches Jerusalem, the heavy influence of the Jewish Christians there causes the Jewish leaders to take issue with Peter upon his return. Peter explains his actions, which, as he demonstrates, are a direct response to the revealed will of God. Peter convincingly describes his conclusion, "If then God gave the same gift to them as he gave to us when we believed in the Lord Jesus Christ, who was I that I could stand in God's way?" (Acts 11:17). Peter's persuasiveness is very effective. Luke describes the response that occurs among the Jewish dominant believers listening to Peter, "When they heard these things they fell silent. And they glorified God, saying, 'Then to the Gentiles also God has granted repentance that leads to life'" (Acts 11:18).

---

8. Italics mine for emphasis.

9. Speaking of Acts chapter 9, eighteenth-century Princeton scholar, J. A. Alexander, writes, "This chapter is entirely occupied with one great subject, the first reception of converted Gentiles to the Church, without passing through the intermediate state of Judaism. To this narrative, 9, 31–43 is an introduction, and 11, 1–18 an appendix." Alexander, *Acts*, 387.

Step Three: "To The Gentiles"

The verse above is not only a critical statement for Luke's purposes, but is, in some ways, the crescendo affirmation for the entire book of Acts. The Gentiles are in! God is not just Jew-oriented. Possibly the most prominent Jew of influence, the Apostle Peter himself, is the advocate of the Gentiles. God has opened the door to the "whole world," and although Peter is not the man to reach the Gentiles on a large scale, he could have been a very large impediment to the mission of incorporating them into Christ's ever expanding kingdom. Nevertheless, he not only advocates for them by stepping away from being an obstacle, he is actually the major leader who helps open the door of the kingdom to the entire Gentile world. These Gentiles believe, receive the Holy Spirit, and are "legitimized" by being baptized in the name of Jesus Christ. We must note that Peter's "conversion" to Gentile acceptance in Acts chapter 10 is sandwiched between Paul's conversion to Christ in Acts chapter 9 and the establishment of the first fully Gentile church as seen in Acts chapter 11. Luke's point is that Peter must be on board or else he might easily be a detriment to Christ's Great Commission. With Peter's wholehearted support of Gentile outreach, the apostle Paul will eventually become the more prominent character presented to us by Luke.

So Send I You

ACT TWO
STEP THREE
"TO THE GENTILES"

PHILIP TO...
AN ETHIOPIAN
SAMARIA
ACTS 8:26-40

SAUL/PAUL
CONVERTED
MESSENGER TO
THE GENTILES
ACTS 9

PETER
OBSTACLE REMOVED
GOSPEL IS FOR
EVERYONE
ACTS 10:1-11-11:18

ACTS 8:26-11:18
Figure Seven

Step Four:
"The First True Church"

In the middle of Acts chapter 11, we find a major shift in Luke's narrative of the expanding church. This shift describes a major break in the unfolding of early church history, and "Buck" Hatch contends that based upon the significance of this turn of events, Acts 11:19 would be worthy of being designated with a chapter division (for example, calling it "Acts chapter 12").

Luke writes,

> 19Now those who were scattered because of the persecution that arose over Stephen traveled as far as Phoenicia and Cyprus and Antioch, speaking the word to no one except Jews. 20 But there were some of them, men of Cyprus and Cyrene, who on coming to Antioch spoke to the Hellenists also, preaching the Lord Jesus. 21 And the hand of the Lord was with them, and a great number who believed turned to the Lord. 22 The report of this came to the ears of the church in Jerusalem, and they sent Barnabas to Antioch. 23 When he came and saw the grace of God, he was glad, and he exhorted them all to remain faithful to the Lord with steadfast purpose, 24 for he was a good man, full of the Holy Spirit and of faith. And a great many people were added to the Lord. 25 So Barnabas went to Tarsus to look for Saul, 26 and when he had found him, he brought him to Antioch. For a whole year they met with the church and taught a great many people. And in Antioch the disciples were first called Christians.[1]

In order to provide some background to the landmark step that is about to occur, Luke returns to the storyline contained in Acts chapter 8 (verse 4) in which the believers in Jerusalem were dispersed due to persecution. They were scattered abroad carrying the gospel with them. However, Luke notes that even though they spread themselves in various and vast directions,

---

1. Acts 11:19–26.

initially they carried the gospel *only* to their own people, the Jews. Luke then notes that "some" of the dispersed went to Antioch (of Syria), a city located on the coast of the Mediterranean Sea, a few hundred miles north of Jerusalem. Antioch was the third largest city in the Roman Empire at this time and contained a large Jewish community.[2] There, these new believers share the gospel with Hellenists (fully Greek or Gentile), an unusual cross-cultural endeavor. The reception is incredible because it is now God's time for the Gentiles to hear the gospel and believe. God's power is made manifest in this god-forsaken city. Many come to faith in Christ, and the impact is obviously so great that the news travels far—all the way back to the church in Jerusalem. In response, the Jerusalem church, recognizes that these new believers need more teaching and training. They determine that this situation is very unique and different, so they decide to send the most encouraging-natured individual possible—the disciple named Barnabas—to travel north and help them.

Luke's text is stunningly and beautifully worded when he writes simply, "Barnabas comes and sees the grace of God and he is happy" (Acts 11:23, paraphrased). What more needs to be said? And the inevitable occurs, as Barnabas, ever gifted to encourage, exhorts these new believers to remain faithful to the Lord whom they have just discovered. Luke does not provide a detailed description of the church except to tell us that through the ministry of Barnabas (and maybe some of the other original gospel proclaimers) many more are added to the Lord (Acts 11:24b). In essence, Gentiles are coming to faith in Christ in growing numbers, and amazing grace is occurring before our very eyes. These numbers are overwhelming and it seems, intuitively, that Barnabas realizes he needs help in order to properly disciple these new believers. He immediately leaves for Tarsus in search of one very valuable and Gentile savvy apostle by the name of Paul. He finds him and brings him back to Antioch for ministry purposes. This gospel driven duo spend an entire year with the church at Antioch, and we can only imagine the teaching, praying, and growing that went on among this fledgling gospel enterprise.

Luke tells us that a great many were taught in the church at Antioch, and that these maturing disciples of Christ were labeled with a name that would characterize believers in Jesus until he returns. They were the first to be called "Christians"; some scholars think that this label was given in derision, as a nickname to mock them. The name "Christian" demonstrates,

---

2. Bruce, *Book of Acts*, 238.

Step Four: "The First True Church"

at the least, that this new church in Antioch, being comprised of primarily Gentile believers, is proof that the community of believers who follow Christ can no longer be considered to be a "Jewish sect." The church at Antioch is now the first pure church, i.e., a church that reflects the mandate of the Great Commission of Christ; it is a church for *the world*. It is localized, has no political associations, and exists in the midst of the contemporary society of the unbelieving pagan culture. The church at Antioch appears to be a mature church, full of new believers formed from the Gentile world. Antioch reflects the great progress that has occurred in the life of the church. The church has moved away from the place of its birth—the womb of Jerusalem—and has continued to grow and expand into both nearby Judea and Samaria, while now having "grown up" and ready to interact with the world of the Gentiles.

The ensuing "footnote" at the end of Acts chapter 11, and the stories in Acts chapter 12, demonstrate that although this growing church is on the move, there are concerns. The "mother" church in Jerusalem is challenged, most probably with impoverishment, and will continue to suffer. A prophet named Agabus foretells of a major famine. The Jerusalem church will need relief and help; Barnabas and Saul—ever the ministering companions—will deliver that help. Herod the king (Agrippa I)[3] kills James, the brother of John (the "sons of thunder," cf. Mark 3:17), who apparently lives in Jerusalem. Then, seeing that he has pleased the Jews with this targeted persecution, Herod goes after Peter and arrests him as well. Peter, however, miraculously escapes his imprisonment. Herod's fate is a subsidiary subject in the chapter, as ultimately he exalts himself as a god among the people after delivering an oration to them. An angel of the Lord strikes him down on the spot and he dies. For Luke, the bottom line of Acts chapter 12 is that despite the first apostolic martyr (James), and the arrest and imprisonment of the chief apostle in Jerusalem (Peter), by the hands of a tyrant king (Herod) ". . . the word of God increased and multiplied" (Acts 12:24). Nothing can stop Christ's church, even as it exists underneath many threatening circumstances.

---

3. Ibid., 246.

ACT TWO
STEP FOUR
"THE FIRST TRUE CHURCH"

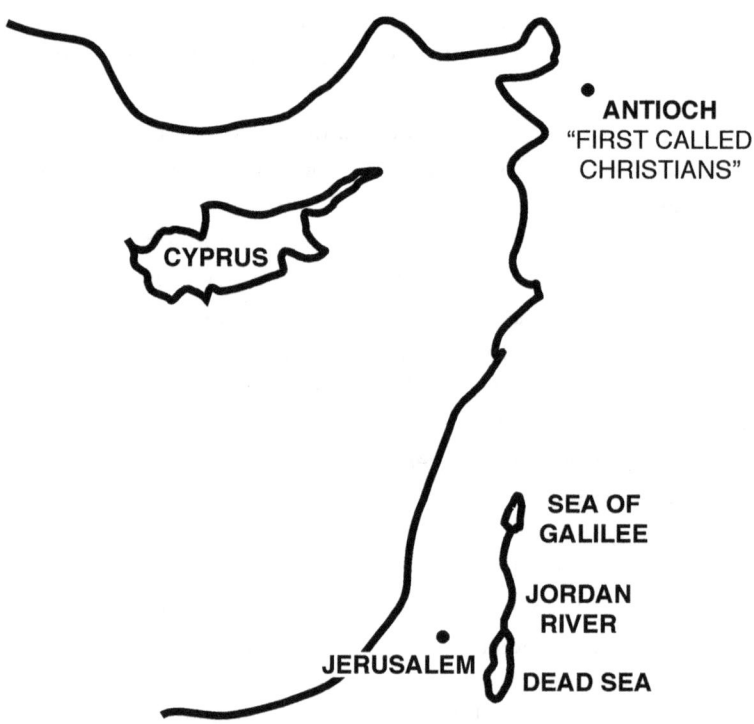

ACTS 11:19-26
Figure Eight

Step Five: "To The World"

THE REMAINDER OF THE book of Acts (or the second half of the book) involves the progress of gospel proclamation "to the end of the earth" (Acts 1:8). Thus far, we have watched it explode in Jerusalem where it creates an incredibly dynamic congregation that thrives in spite of, and possibly due to, local resistance and persecution. At the height of persecution, and in the face of the threat of death, these early Jewish believers are dispersed to the surrounding communities, both Judea and Samaria. But Christ their Lord has a vision of the proclamation of world-wide grace for all of the peoples and nations on the globe. He dramatically converts Saul/Paul who will be his instrument for Gentile evangelism, paves the way for this endeavor by convincing the very Jewish Peter that inclusion of the Gentiles has always been a part of his divine plan, and initiates a fully Gentile church in Antioch.

In review—and to enable us to visualize what is happening—I will use three metaphors to describe this gospel progress. We noted that in the first seven chapters of the book of Acts (step one), we saw the proclamation of the gospel in and around Jerusalem, beginning in the temple area. Luke describes the church's growth, as if she is *a snowball rolling downhill*, constantly adding new believers and members, increasing in size. Christ's followers become a seeming threat to the local Jewish religious leaders, including a chief antagonist by the name of Saul. Step two (Acts 8:1) describes the persecution of the church, a hostility that thrusts the believers in all directions, throughout Judea, Galilee, and Samaria. The believers are scattered like *cats fleeing a loud commotion*. The church is now reaching the surrounding areas of Jerusalem, but still must *go* to the world! Steps three and four explain how God raises up Paul, his apostle to the Gentile world, and how Peter is schooled by God to realize that the kingdom is intended not only for the Jews, but includes the despised Gentiles as well. The growing snowball has now been "scared" into dispersion and the book of Acts, from chapter 13 until the end of the book, will now appear more like *the diary of a travelogue* than a growing, rolling snowball.

The primary purpose of this book is simply to provide a short narrative of the growth of the New Testament church through some basic concepts. The last half of the book of Acts includes so much information that it forbids me from explaining the necessary information to cover each and every journey. Elaborating on all of the historical, geographical, and sociological contexts would make the travelogue quite burdensome.[1] However, we do want to watch the gospel and its proclaimers travel and thrive throughout the book of Acts. As the narrative unfolds, we will observe how Luke builds his case for the validity of this new movement. Acts serves as a defense—an apologetic—of the Holy Spirit's involvement in the life of the early church and her apostles. Luke also writes because he has not only been converted by the good news of Christ, but has gotten caught up in the progression of the church's chief proponent to the Gentiles, the Apostle Paul. F.F. Bruce declares, "For Paul no doubt is Luke's hero."[2]

Missionary Journey One—Acts 13:1-14:28

Step five consists of four different gospel-driven journeys. Luke begins with the account of the first missionary journey, one initiated by the newly established "Christian" church located in Antioch (Acts 13:1-14:28). Indeed, the first "missions minded" church consists of converted Gentiles (such as Luke himself) who see the need to take the gospel to other Gentiles who haven't yet heard it (as they have). This outreach is a movement of the Holy Spirit and occurs in the context of a church doing ministry, along with the practice of fasting. When the Holy Spirit instructs the church to "Set apart for me Barnabas and Saul for the work to which I have called them" in Acts 13:2, the church responds by more fasting, prayer, and laying hands on these two designated servants. The year is probably 47-48 AD.[3] They travel by sea, going southwest of Antioch through the Mediterranean, first landing at a large island called Cyprus. Strategically speaking, Cyprus is Barnabas's homeland (Acts 4:36). We can imagine Barnabas telling Paul (whose new name is clarified by Luke in Acts 13:9), "I know where I want

---

1. Thankfully, there are many good commentaries that one can read to find material which will enlighten the reader in the travelogue. See a list of authors in the bibliography.

2. Bruce, *Acts*, 26.

3. These and subsequent dates are taken from this link: https://www.christianitytoday.com/history/issues/issue-47/apostle-paul-and-his-times-christian-history-timeline.html)

Step Five: "To The World"

us to go first!" They focus on the Jewish synagogues hoping for open audiences on the island. From Cyprus, they visit a number of cities in the area known as Galatia. The most significant event mentioned by Luke is Paul's synagogue sermon in a city called Pisidian Antioch. Paul once again enters a synagogue and after reading the Scriptures (the Law and the Prophets), the synagogue officials actually request that he speak. What an open door this synagogue appears to be! Paul preaches a sermon that summarizes the Old Testament narrative and underscores the death of Christ, as well as his resurrection. He concludes with these words of gospel invitation,

> 38 Let it be known to you therefore, brothers, that through this man forgiveness of sins is proclaimed to you, 39 and by him everyone who believes is freed from everything from which you could not be freed by the law of Moses. 40 Beware, therefore, lest what is said in the Prophets should come about: 41 'Look, you scoffers, be astounded and perish; for I am doing a work in your days, a work that you will not believe, even if one tells it to you.'[4]

Paul is then invited to return and address the synagogue on the next Sabbath. He also gains a small following of interested Jew and Gentile converts to Judaism and urges them to continue in the grace of God.

The very next Sabbath is action packed! Crowds swell to hear Paul, but the local Jews jealously contradict his words and heap abuse on him. However, such resistance will not deter this grace loving apostle. He is emboldened to preach once again. This sermon is the highlight of the first missionary journey. Paul is pressed to announce the greatest news that the world will ever hear. He boldly asserts the message of God's expansive kingdom for the first time:

> 46 And Paul and Barnabas spoke out boldly, saying, "It was necessary that the word of God be spoken first to you. Since you thrust it aside and judge yourselves unworthy of eternal life, behold, we are turning to the Gentiles. 47 For so the Lord has commanded us, saying, "'I have made you a light for the Gentiles, that you may bring salvation to the ends of the earth.'"[5]

Luke wraps up this grand account with three compelling observations:

1. "And when the Gentiles heard this, they began rejoicing and glorifying the word of the Lord, and as many as were appointed to eternal life believed." (13:48)

---

4. Acts 13:38–41.
5. Acts 13:46–47.

2. "And the word of the Lord was spreading throughout the whole region." (13:49)

3. "And the disciples were filled with joy and with the Holy Spirit." (13:52)

Luke's summary demonstrates that Paul's preaching of the gospel is being blessed by God. Gentiles are definitely being included in God's plan—they are chosen to receive it—and the Holy Spirit is being poured out on the disciples. Most significant is the excitement and conversion of the Gentiles. The snow ball is rolling outside of Jerusalem and Judea, and is gaining momentum in the world.

Acts chapter 14 is a continuation of the first missionary journey, and Luke highlights these visits by noting the following:

1. In the synagogue at Iconium, Paul and Barnabas "spoke in such a way that a great number of both Jews and Greeks believed" (Acts 14:1).

2. Crowds and multitudes continue to listen to the gospel message (Acts 14:4, 11, 18, 19) but not with full understanding (the evangelistic duo are seen as being Greek gods), nor acceptance (Paul is almost stoned to death).

3. ". . . and on the next day he went on with Barnabas to Derbe. 21 When they had preached the gospel to that city and had made many disciples, they returned to Lystra and to Iconium and to Antioch, 22 strengthening the souls of the disciples, encouraging them to continue in the faith, and saying that through many tribulations we must enter the kingdom of God" (Acts 14:20–21).

4. The missionary team appoints elders in every church, indicating that multiple churches have been planted and that they have men committed enough to Christ that they can lead the churches.

5. The missionary team returns to Antioch—their home base—and upon arrival, they gather the church together and report about "all that God had done through them and how he had opened a door of faith to the Gentiles" (Acts 14:27).

We can only imagine how the stories of gospel proclamation, gospel reception, and life threatening gospel persecution impacted the believers at Antioch. Along with the organization of new churches filled with Jewish converts, and especially Gentile believers, the congregation gathered together at Antioch must have been thrilled. God is at work, using willing servants and a message of Christ's death and resurrection to reach the world! What could be better than that?

A Bump in the Mission Enterprise—Acts 15

As unbelievable as the inclusion of the Gentiles in God's plan may seem, not everyone is happy about it. In Acts chapter 15, we see the creation of a major obstacle. Luke notes, in the first two verses, that the early church is facing two key problems:

1. Jewish Christian leaders (probably converted Pharisees) who are holding onto their past Judaism, as well as to their allegiance to Moses and Mosaic law, create a major problem in the burgeoning church. They insist on the Jewish rite of circumcision in order for a person to be saved. Their law-bent position necessitates that the newly believing Gentiles must add a Jewish rite to the grace they have received in Christ. They are teaching that circumcision is necessary for salvation. This issue presents a major crisis to the future of the church.

2. Secondly, since the Gentiles who have responded to the gospel message of the first missionary journey are uncircumcised, the Jewish church is being forced to make a decision regarding the reception and/or inclusion of those Gentiles into the church. They are no longer dealing with the obscure conversion of the Ethiopian eunuch (Acts 8:26–40), or a Roman centurion and his family (Acts 10), but with the mass conversion of Gentiles entering the church through Paul's first evangelistic excursion.

A council consisting of the apostles and others is called to discuss this pressing "circumcision" problem. They hold the meeting in Jerusalem, most probably occurring in 49 AD. The bottom line is presented by a persuaded Peter, who takes the lead and, of course, argues that all—both Jew and Gentile—are "saved through grace" (Acts 15:11). Paul and Barnabas provide testimony, verifying what God is doing among the Gentiles. The meeting crescendos with James, leader of the Jerusalem church, and a strict, law abiding Jew, contending that the prophets (Amos 9:11–12) themselves also concur with Peter's conclusion that God is calling the Gentiles into his program for the world.

These various church leaders—apostles and elders—come to an agreement and decide to communicate their conclusion, in letter form, to their brothers (a warm and affirmative designation) in Antioch and beyond. They write the following:

> 23 The brothers, both the apostles and the elders, to the brothers who are of the Gentiles in Antioch and Syria and Cilicia, greetings. 24 Since we have heard that some persons have gone out from us and troubled you with words, unsettling your minds, although we gave them no instructions, 25 it has seemed good to us, having come to one accord, to choose men and send them to you with our beloved Barnabas and Paul, 26 men who have risked their lives for the name of our Lord Jesus Christ. 27 We have therefore sent Judas and Silas, who themselves will tell you the same things by word of mouth. 28 For it has seemed good to the Holy Spirit and to us to lay on you no greater burden than these requirements: 29 that you abstain from what has been sacrificed to idols, and from blood, and from what has been strangled, and from sexual immorality. If you keep yourselves from these, you will do well. Farewell.[6]

Upon receiving this correspondence, the congregation at Antioch rejoices due to its encouraging words. Grace has prevailed! The scruples that could prevent "table fellowship" between Jews and Gentiles are addressed. These leaders prescribe certain prohibitions, including associations with idol worship, meat containing blood, and improper sexual relations (i.e., requiring non-conformity to the low standards of pagan sexual practices).[7] Luke tells us that Judas and Silas also speak encouraging words to the believers there, thus strengthening them. Furthermore, Paul and Barnabas remain in Antioch, where they and many others teach and preach the word of the Lord.

The key point to this chapter is that the conflict—and potential for division—among the flourishing church has been resolved. Jews are not only receiving the newly converted Gentiles into the church, but they are growing in their own understanding of God's grace. The church is united and there is peace among her members. A possible doctrinal hurricane has been averted and the winds of grace are blowing among God's people. More Gentiles must be reached by the glorious message of forgiveness through the cross and resurrection of the Lord Jesus Christ.

---

6. Acts 15:23b–29.
7. Bruce, *Book of Acts*, 311.

Step Five: "To The World"
Missionary Journey Two—Acts 15:36–18:22

After the tempestuous waters of the Jerusalem council have receded, due to its successful resolution, Paul and Barnabas decide to return and visit the churches that they had previously planted in the first missionary journey. This journey covers the years 49–52 AD. Highlights of this lengthy journey include the following:

1. Paul discovers Timothy, who becomes a dear son in the faith and partner in Paul's ministry (Acts 16:3).

2. The decrees passed down from the Jerusalem council are delivered, with the very positive response (again, remember that Luke is writing a defense for the church), "So the churches were strengthened in the faith, and they increased in numbers daily" (Acts16:5).

3. The church at Philippi blossoms through three individual encounters with the evangelists: a woman who deals in purple cloth is converted (the first believer on the European continent), a fortune-telling female slave (who is apparently converted), and a jailer who believes, along with his whole household (Acts 16).

4. In Thessalonica, after Paul preaches on the resurrection of Christ, we read, "And some of them were persuaded and joined Paul and Silas, as did a great many of the devout Greeks and not a few of the leading women (Acts 17:4). However, subsequently, Paul is run out of town (Acts 17:10).

5. In Berea, when Paul enters the Jewish synagogue, the Berean listeners diligently examine the Scriptures with him. Luke writes, "Many of them therefore believed, with not a few Greek women of high standing as well as men." Some antagonistic Jews come from Thessalonica and Paul is once more run out of town (Acts 17:12,14).

6. In Athens, Paul is all alone and surrounded by idols. He preaches a sermon using a philosophical approach; Luke describes the response, "Now when they heard of the resurrection of the dead, some mocked. But others said, 'We will hear you again about this.' 33 So Paul went out from their midst. 34 But some men joined him and believed, among whom also were Dionysius the Areopagite and a woman named Damaris and others with them" (Acts 17:32–34).

7. In Corinth, Paul enters a city known for its idolatry and immorality. His message is rejected by the Jews. He then declares a ministry defining statement to these abusive Jews, "Your blood be on your own heads! I am innocent. From now on I will go to the Gentiles" (Acts 18:6). However, Crispus, the synagogue leader, believes along with his household, and many native Corinthians believe as well and are baptized (Acts 18:8).

8. Paul makes a short stay in Ephesus, but promises to return, if the Lord wills (Acts 18:19–21).

9. Paul winds up his second missionary journey by going to Caesarea and then down to Antioch where his journey ends. He finishes a trip of approximately three years and twenty-eight hundred miles.

Missionary Journey Three—Acts 18:23–21:16

The third missionary journey appears to be motivated, at least partially, by Paul's promise to return to the city of Ephesus. The time period covers 53–57 AD. Highlights of this journey include the following:

1. Paul passes through Galatia and Phrygia and then lands once more in Ephesus. Some of John the Baptist's disciples there believe and receive the Holy Spirit (Acts 19:1–7). Paul spends three months in the synagogues of Ephesus, but because of opposition, he withdraws for two years to the school (or lecture hall) of a local teacher named Tyrannus (Acts 19:8–10).[8] Through his ministry, many believe, are marvelously converted, and the Lord's word prevails. Luke notes, "So the word of the Lord continued to increase and prevail mightily" (Acts 19:20). It is here, in Ephesus, that Paul writes his *first letter to the church at Corinth*.

2. Paul has a vision to get the gospel to the city of Rome (Acts 19:21). Eventually, however, a local silversmith named Demetrius, who makes silver shrines, causes a commotion that once again drives Paul out of the region (Acts 19:22–41).

3. In Macedonia (Acts 20:1), Paul writes his *second letter to the church at Corinth*.

---

8. Ibid., 388.

Step Five: "To The World"

4. In Greece (Acts 20:2), Paul writes his landmark work, *the letter to the church at Rome* (55–57 AD).

5. Luke joins Paul in his travels, as noted by the use of the first person personal pronouns, "we" and "us," (Acts 20:5).

6. After various other stops, Paul arrives at the city of Miletus. In his rush to arrive at Jerusalem for the celebration of Pentecost,[9] he has bypassed Ephesus. However, from Miletus, he calls together the elders of the Ephesian church and gives them a moving message, reminding them of his ministry with them, and exhorting them to guard the flock. The touching scene closes with praying, weeping, embracing, kissing, and grieving (Acts 20:17–38). Perhaps Luke's stirring account of Paul's parting message to the elders of Ephesus is written as an example of church oversight for all of the churches that Paul has previously founded.

7. Paul continues to travel and when he lands in the city of Tyre, the disciples there tell him, through the Spirit, not to continue on to Jerusalem (Acts 21:3).

8. Eventually, Paul ends up in Caesarea, where he stays with Philip the evangelist (Acts 21:8; cf. Acts 8:5–40). Agabas (cf. Acts 11:28) predicts that Paul will be bound by the Jews in Jerusalem and delivered to the Gentiles (Acts 21:11). Despite a multitude of pleas by the disciples, Paul resolutely replies, "What are you doing, weeping and breaking my heart? For I am ready not only to be imprisoned but even to die in Jerusalem for the name of the Lord Jesus" (Acts 21:13).

Paul finally arrives at Jerusalem (57–59 AD) and, technically speaking, his missionary journeys are finished (Acts 21:17). However, one last journey remains and his ministry is far from complete. He will move from testifying of Christ to the masses of Europe to proclaiming Christ to some major political leaders who need to hear this world-wide message of hope and forgiveness.

---

9. "It has been disputed whether this desire had reference to the observation of the feast or the multitudes gathered at it." Alexander, *Acts*, 238.

The Journey to Rome (Paul's Captivities and Gospel Proclamations)—Acts 21:17-28:31

Jerusalem Captivity (Acts 21:17–23:32)

Paul arrives at Jerusalem (57–59 AD) and receives a warm welcome from the believers there, including James and the elders at the church. He provides an exciting missionary report, explaining to these Jewish believers in detail about how God has worked among the Gentiles. His report results in great praise to God. Concern for both the law and local Jewish Christians prompts Paul to enter the temple with some of his companions in order to purify himself. However, while at the temple some Jews from the province of Asia falsely accuse Paul of bringing Greeks into the temple, thus defiling it. Paul is seized by the tempestuous crowd, beaten with intent to kill, and saved only by Roman intervention (Acts 21:27–40).

Through some quick negotiation with the Roman soldiers, he is able to speak to the crowd. He is a captive with an audience (Acts 22:1–21). *Paul presents his first defense—the gospel is proclaimed before a Jewish crowd.* As Paul shares his story (his testimony) his listeners appear engaged until he mentions a certain trigger phrase, "And he said to me, 'Go, for I will send you far away to the Gentiles.'" This comment incenses the crowd and they go from engaged to enraged (Acts 22:21–23). Paul, however, is spared from Roman scourging by appealing to his Roman citizenship (Acts 22:23–30).

Paul is then able to *present his second defense—the resurrection is proclaimed before the Jewish Sanhedrin (religious council).* Knowing that the Sanhedrin consists of both Pharisees, who believe in the resurrection, and Sadducees, who do not believe in the resurrection, Paul cunningly divides the Council over this issue. The chaos leads to his return to the prison barracks. One night later, surmising that Paul might be despondent and dejected, Luke tells us, "The following night the Lord stood by him and said, 'Take courage, for as you have testified to the facts about me in Jerusalem, so you must testify also in Rome'" (Acts 23:11).

Caesarean Captivity (Acts 23:33–26:32)

Despite death threats and the promise of an ambush by forty Jews, Paul is delivered through the safe escort of two hundred Roman soldiers who take him to Governor Felix in the city of Caesarea. He is housed, under guard,

Step Five: "To the World"

in King Herod's palace. Paul then stands trial and is able to *present his third defense—the resurrection and judgment are proclaimed before the Roman imperial governor, Felix.* He is able to defend his innocence, explain that his message resonates with the Law and the Prophets, and with boldness declare that there will certainly be a resurrection of both the righteous and the wicked. However, Felix eventually brings his young (and third) wife Drusilla,[10] who was Jewish, to hear Paul proclaim his faith in Christ, and decides to leave Paul in prison for two years as a favor to the Jews. Paul becomes a toy with which Felix might play, in hopes of gaining money from this intriguing prisoner. Known for his dishonesty and immorality, as well as being a ruthless tyrant,[11] Felix hopes only to keep the Jews under his charge happy, while maintaining no sense of true justice for the Apostle Paul.

Eventually, Festus arrives as the new governor who would replace Felix. With his appearance the Jews attempt to exploit him due to his inexperience.[12] They thus present Paul's case to him, looking for a means to rid themselves of this trouble maker. Festus travels to Caesarea and Paul is called forth to testify (59–60 AD). The Apostle is now able to *present his fourth defense—the truthfulness of his ministry is proclaimed before another Roman imperial governor, Festus.* The Apostle Paul declares his legal innocence with regard to both the Jews and Rome. Festus, attempting to appease the Jews, asks Paul if he would like to defend himself in Jerusalem. In order to save his life (which would be endangered by a trip to Jerusalem), Paul wisely retrieves his one "ace in the hole" in order to prevail. Using his Roman citizenship, he appeals to Caesar. Festus confers with his council and declares, "You have appealed to Caesar. To Caesar you will go!" (Acts 25:12). Soon, Paul will be "on to Rome," the city where he aspires to take the gospel.

In the meantime, King Agrippa, King of Judea[13] and his wife, Bernice, visit Caesarea and pay their respects to the new governor, Festus. Festus, knowing that he will have to justify his actions when he sends Paul to Rome (Acts 25:26), explains his conundrum with Paul to Agrippa in order to gain his counsel. With much pomp and circumstance, Paul is brought forth to

10. Bruce, *Book of Acts*, 472–3.
11. Alexander, *Acts*, 376.
12. Bruce, *Book of Acts*, 475.
13. "This man was the son of Herod Agrippa I, king of Judea from A.D. 41 to 44; cf. Acts 12:1." Ibid., 481.

speak. In Acts chapter 26, Luke records the speech of speeches (or sermon of sermons) given by the Apostle Paul. With great diplomacy, Paul unfolds both his personal testimony of meeting the resurrected Christ, along with his call to gospel ministry. He is able to *present his fifth defense—the sufferings of Christ and his resurrection from the dead are proclaimed to the King of Judea.* In mid-sentence, while Paul is stating his mission—Christ to the Jews and also to the Gentiles—King Agrippa interrupts the Apostle, accusing him of insanity. In reply, Paul attempts to persuade Agrippa to come to Christ, demonstrating that both Paul and his arguments are quite sane. Ultimately, Luke fulfills his goal of delivering an apologetical defense for the gospel and the church it has spawned when he writes,

> 30 Then the king rose, and the governor and Bernice and those who were sitting with them. 31 And when they had withdrawn, they said to one another, "This man is doing nothing to deserve death or imprisonment." 32 And Agrippa said to Festus, "This man could have been set free if he had not appealed to Caesar."[14]

Luke affirms that neither this "new Jewish cult," nor its prominent leader, are violating Jewish law and tradition, nor are they in violation of Roman law. In many ways, Acts chapter 26 is the crescendo of the book. The gospel of Christ and his resurrection has been defended and proclaimed from the streets of Jerusalem up to the King of Judea. And in doing so, the true King of Judah, Jesus Christ, to whom both the law and prophets testify, has been announced from the hills of Judah to the throne of Judea. And let the record state—the message is without heresy and is free from the guilt of the false accusations of the Jews.

Roman Captivity (Acts 27–28)

In Luke's account, the trip to Italy describes Paul as a prisoner among fellow prisoners travelling on a ship under Roman centurion guard. The journey includes a number of stops, a change of ships, some health care for Paul, and some stormy, life-threatening weather that leads Paul to predict an inevitable ship wreck. The wreck occurs (with Luke, the dramatist story teller and historian milking it for all it was worth) and everyone—276 persons—survives. The Apostle Paul shines forth, trusting, acknowledging, and thanking God in and through all of these navigational trials.

---

14. Acts 26:30–32.

Step Five: "To The World"

Having literally jumped ship and floated to land using planks and other pieces of the ship's cargo, the group of passengers discover that they have found refuge on an island called Malta. All of their lives, including of course the life of the primary character in the story, have been spared by providence. Nevertheless, Luke retains a story that demonstrates the extraordinary hand of God on the apostle. Paul is bitten by a venomous viper that has been driven out of the heated firewood, but simply shakes it off, continuing as though nothing has happened (much to the consternation of the superstitious Maltese islanders). In response to this incident, however, the news gets out among the Maltese people. Those suffering from disease flock to Paul with hopes of healing, and many are cured (Acts 28:1-10).

The journey to Rome continues uneventfully and Paul finally arrives at his cherished destination (Acts 28:16). Under house arrest, and guarded by Roman centurions, the apostle freely preaches the Lord Jesus Christ to the Jews, who reject his message (Acts 28:17-27), and then to all who will hear. Luke makes the point that Paul believes that the gospel is for the whole world, "Therefore let it be known to you that this salvation of God has been sent to the Gentiles; they will listen" (Acts 28:28). Paul's ministry in Rome lasts for a period of two years (60-62 AD). Here in Rome, Paul *pens the epistles to both Philemon and the Colossians,* as well as the letters to *the Ephesians and the Philippians.* Their compilation under these circumstances provides their characterization as "the prison epistles" of Paul.

Luke concludes his historical account of Paul's existence with these words: "He lived there two whole years at his own expense, and welcomed all who came to him, 31 proclaiming the kingdom of God and teaching about the Lord Jesus Christ with all boldness and without hindrance" (Acts 28:30-31). Luke's grand account of "the gospel from Jerusalem to Rome" is finally complete and ends with a triumphant climax and conclusion for the reader: Rome poses no obstacles to the preaching of Christ. Even if the apostle to the Gentiles is imprisoned, the gospel is not.

We might further note that, although Luke does not record it, during a brief release from his two-year house arrest (62-64 AD), the Apostle Paul *writes his first letter to Timothy,* who is a pastor to the church in Ephesus. He also *writes a letter of pastoral guidance to Titus,* who is serving as a pastor in Crete (63 AD). Upon being re-imprisoned and just prior to his martyrdom by Rome, Paul writes the stirring and heartrending *second letter to his son in the faith, Timothy* (64 AD). To the reader, the book of Acts might appear to contain a truncated ending, since Luke does not account for the final fate of the Apostle Paul. But in Luke's mind (even if Paul is his hero), the life of Paul remains secondary to the author's portrayal of the progress of the good news of the Lord Jesus Christ and his kingdom. Jesus triumphs from Jerusalem to Rome and beyond!

ACT TWO
STEP FIVE
"TO THE WORLD"

FIRST MISSIONARY JOURNEY	JERUSALEM COUNCIL	SECOND MISSIONARY JOURNEY	THIRD MISSIONARY JOURNEY	JOURNEY TO ROME
				1. JERUSALEM CAPTIVITY 21:17-23:32
				2. CAESAREAN CAPTIVITY 23:33-26:32
				3. ROMAN CAPTIVITY 27-28
13:1-14:28	15	15:36-18:22	18:23-21:16	21:17-28:31

ACTS 13:1-28:31
Figure Nine

Conclusion

Review

WE HAVE WATCHED THE Great Commission of Jesus Christ unfold before our very eyes. Luke's version of the Christ's Great Commission is stated at the beginning of the book of Acts, "But you will receive power when the Holy Spirit has come upon you, and you will be my witnesses in Jerusalem and in all Judea and Samaria, and to the end of the earth" (Acts 1:8). Luke has accomplished his task of describing act two in God's progress of redemption. In act one we saw God plant a seed through the promise to Abraham and create a redemptive channel, i.e., a nation of people who would live in "the place" designated for sacrifice. Jerusalem is the place where men and women, as well as children, can find acceptance and come to know God through the sacrificial system (appeasing God through atonement for sin). Even when the channel of redemption appears to be utterly destroyed (through both Assyrian and Babylonian invasion and captivity), God graciously brings a remnant of his people back to the Promised Land. Although restored in time, this remnant once again drifts away from God in rebellion and compromise, but God is faithful.

He sends his son, Jesus—whose name means "Yahweh Saves." Atonement (satisfaction for God's wrath upon sin)—perfect and complete—is finished through the sinless life and unblemished sacrifice of Christ on the cross. After being put to death, Christ is raised to life, proving that God the Father is pleased with his son's atoning work. "It is finished"—Christ's work is sufficient for the world. After the resurrection, Jesus appears a number of times to his disciples, and just before ascending into the heavens to reign at his father's right hand in glory, meets with and promises them that they will receive the power of the Holy Spirit; he will enable them to take the good news of God's forgiveness to the world. That promise is seen in act two of God's redemptive plan. It begins with the stories which Luke conveys in the book of Acts and continues as the true church of God proclaims the glory of God, the Son, to the world. All we need to be saved from the darkness of this world is repentance toward God and faith in Jesus Christ (Acts 20:21).

Act two is the fulfillment of the second aspect of the original promise made to Abraham in Genesis 12:1–3. God will surely use Abraham and his descendants to bless the entire world. Indeed, God had promised, "and in you all the families of the earth shall be blessed" and through Christ's work and Great Commission, the Lord God has kept his promise. Today the gospel is being proclaimed throughout the entire world and the light of God is shining into the darkness. May it continue to shine brightly, and may the gospel radiate in all of those places where the darkness remains.

One Verse

If the reader hasn't guessed it yet, there is one verse (actually half of one verse) in Scripture that summarizes the entire Bible—one verse alone. It consists of a short sentence by Jesus, but encompasses both of the books I have written that explain God's grand redemptive plan. In John chapter 20, after his resurrection, Jesus comes to be with some of his disciples who are trembling together in a room of locked doors, afraid of possible Jewish persecution. He speaks to them with what appears to be softly encouraging words. Twice he says, "Peace be with you." Then, in twelve simple words[1] *he encapsulates the entire Bible*, summarizing both acts one and two when he says, "As the Father has sent me, even so I am sending you" (John 20:21).[2] One verse says it all. The Father sends the Son to redeem the world; the Son sends us to tell his message of redemption to the world. May *we* be a part of God's unfolding drama of redemption, wherever we find ourselves today.

Where are you?

I don't know if you are like me, but I don't go to the mall very often. There are usually too many stores, too many temptations, and not enough money (and during the Christmas season, too many people). I still remember, however, the very first mall that was built in my hometown of Greenville,

---

1. In the English Standard Version.

2. It is an interesting note to see the gospel encapsulated in Acts 20:21, and God's redemptive plan encapsulated in John 20:21—possibly a similarity that will assist the reader in remembering concepts contained within the book.

CONCLUSION

South Carolina in the early 1960s. The property upon which it was built had been owned by my late uncle, John Bolt Culbertson. My Uncle John's red brick home, which I visited as a small child, was located there. He sold the property (probably for a pretty penny) and the construction crews razed his home. In time, a company built this unique shopping edifice, which was called the Wade Hampton Mall Shopping Center. The Wade Hampton Mall was relatively small, but did contain around twenty stores, and better yet, had a movie theater adjacent to it. And although it was not an "indoor" mall, no one cared. We had never had a mall before! That mall was an amazing addition to my growing and expanding hometown, especially as the city moved eastward. We loved the novelty of the Wade Hampton Mall, as well as the convenience of it. But it was soon to be surpassed by more elaborate and larger malls, first, by one known as McAlister's Square, which was indoor, and better yet, included our first taste of Chick-Fil-A. Then there were even larger malls being built further east, as that side of town continued to expand. Eventually, we enjoyed the Haywood Mall and then Greenville Mall, both huge indoor malls, anchored by large, well-known national retail department stores. I wondered, "How large and diversified could a mall become?" That question was answered once our family moved to the city of Charlotte many years later. Charlotte is a regional city distinguished by a number of malls, two of which have multi-state reputations. One mall, Concord Mills, is a state-of-the-art contemporary mall, covering 1.4 million square feet. Opening in 1999, Concord Mills contained two hundred stores, fifteen anchor tenant stores, a movie theater, and more. At one time it was Charlotte's largest tourist attraction and the number one destination spot for the state of North Carolina. Unimaginable. The other enterprise, South Park Mall, located just a few minutes from the uptown Charlotte area, is an upscale mall, seemingly designed for the affluent who live in southeast Charlotte. South Park Mall only has approximately 145 stores and six anchor tenants, but it is a very impressive mall in every way. South Park Mall contains 1.79 million square feet, so it is very large.

I write these details in order to help the reader think about their own visits to one of those gargantuan malls. What does it mean to stroll the mall? More importantly, what does it mean to look for something that you need at the mall? Where do you start? How do you find the way to that elusive store that you are certain exists, but have no idea *where* it exists? If you have ever explored a huge shopping mall, the answer is clear. You first try to find a mall directory or an indoor map of the mall. (I am told that there are now GPS indoor maps for guidance through maze-like malls.) When you find the directory, what is the first thing you look for? You want to know your present location. Most mall directories point out the location of that directory with some very clear words, often written in bright red. Those words are "You Are Here!" And next to the words the mall explorer will find a huge red arrow pointing out his/her present spot in the mall. So, what is the point? After reading about the unfolding drama of Christ's New Testament church in his drama of redemption, and knowing that God is still at work (building his kingdom of righteousness here on the earth) no matter where you might find yourself in the drama (as you read this book), I can assure you that as you look at this vast world in which we live, there is a big red arrow pointing out the reality that in God's plan, "You Are Here!" You are living right in the midst of God's drama. You have a part to play in Christ's Great Commission. You have a calling from Christ your Lord to proclaim the gospel and make disciples. Where are you? Today, you can humbly bow before the sovereign king of the universe, yield your life to him and be used in his great plan. What a privilege and a purpose! May you see both yourself and your place in the midst of God's unfolding drama today and do all you can to declare his glory among the nations.

Appendix

Israel's Rejection of the Gospel

I WANT TO CONSIDER the sad reality that not only have God's chosen people, the nation of Israel, displayed an historical pattern of resistance and rejection to God's call to be his people, but more so, the sending of Jesus to be their messiah has not curbed their obstinance and darkness. The growth and persecution in the early pages of Acts takes place in the vicinity of the Jerusalem temple. In essence, this movement is Jewish in nature, and though the gospel is consistently presented to various Jewish leaders, those leaders constantly try to squash it. God is proclaiming his son to his beloved people; they are being blessed with the message of the messiah, the one who has been crucified for the sins of his people, and who has been raised in victory over death and sin. Yet the religious leaders of the day, located in the strategic city of Jerusalem (*the place* of temple sacrifice), are entirely missing the good news of the gospel. "He came to his own, and his own people did not receive him" (John 1:11). Sadly, there is no greater irony occurring during this exciting chapter of growth for the New Testament church. Israel, to whom Jesus was sent first (Matt 15:24) is experiencing a gradation of spiritual hardening. It seems that, as a nation, the more they hear, the more they reject their messiah. As time goes by, the religious leaders increase their resistance and become a picture of Israel's rejection of God's promised deliverer, a rejection that will benefit the Gentiles until Israel's future return to faith (Rom 11:25–28). We can follow the development of these rejections, as the gospel makes progress in its proclamation throughout the book of Acts. I will set forth the sections of Acts in chronological order to ensure that we may follow this discouraging hardening of Jewish hearts as they are exposed to the good news of their messiah.

Appendix

Chapter 2

5 Now there were dwelling in Jerusalem Jews, devout men from every nation under heaven. 6 And at this sound the multitude came together, and they were bewildered, because each one was hearing them speak in his own language. 7 And they were amazed and astonished, saying, "Are not all these who are speaking Galileans? 8 And how is it that we hear, each of us in his own native language? 9 Parthians and Medes and Elamites and residents of Mesopotamia, Judea and Cappadocia, Pontus and Asia, 10 Phrygia and Pamphylia, Egypt and the parts of Libya belonging to Cyrene, and visitors from Rome, 11 both Jews and proselytes, Cretans and Arabians—we hear them telling in our own tongues the mighty works of God." 12 And all were amazed and perplexed, saying to one another, "What does this mean?" 13 But others mocking said, "They are filled with new wine."[1]

Note: The falling of the Holy Spirit at Pentecost begins in the context of the temple of Jerusalem. Jews from all over the world hear about the mighty works of God in their own dialect. Yet, others mock the power of God being displayed right before their eyes and ears!

Chapter 4

And as they were speaking to the people, the priests and the captain of the temple and the Sadducees came upon them, 2 greatly annoyed because they were teaching the people and proclaiming in Jesus the resurrection from the dead. 3 And they arrested them and put them in custody until the next day, for it was already evening.

... 17 But in order that it may spread no further among the people, let us warn them to speak no more to anyone in this name." 18 So they called them and charged them not to speak or teach at all in the name of Jesus.[2]

Note: Having healed a lame man in the temple area, Peter preaches a very pointed sermon explaining that the Jews, through the hands of Pilate, have put to death God's Son, who is now risen. Peter shows that Christ fulfills the prophecies of Old Testament prophets, but his message leads to an arrest at

1. Acts 2:5–13.
2. Acts 4:1–3; Acts 4:17–18.

Appendix

the hands of the Jewish religious leaders. These leaders mandate that Peter and John no longer preach in the name of Jesus. The mocking of chapter 2 escalates into major opposition by Jewish authorities (Persecution #1).

Chapter 5

17 But the high priest rose up, and all who were with him (that is, the party of the Sadducees), and filled with jealousy 18 they arrested the apostles and put them in the public prison.

. . . 27 And when they had brought them, they set them before the council. And the high priest questioned them, 28 saying, "We strictly charged you not to teach in this name, yet here you have filled Jerusalem with your teaching, and you intend to bring this man's blood upon us." 29 But Peter and the apostles answered, "We must obey God rather than men. 30 The God of our fathers raised Jesus, whom you killed by hanging him on a tree. 31 God exalted him at his right hand as Leader and Savior, to give repentance to Israel and forgiveness of sins. 32 And we are witnesses to these things, and so is the Holy Spirit, whom God has given to those who obey him." 33 When they heard this, they were enraged and wanted to kill them.

. . . 40 And when they had called in the apostles, they beat them and charged them not to speak in the name of Jesus, and let them go.[3]

Note: The apostles continue to preach (and do wonders) in the temple area (Solomon's portico) and many are coming to the Lord. The Jewish high priest, along with the Sadducees, arrests Peter and other apostles out of jealousy and put them in prison. This event describes the second stage of persecution: testing (Persecution #2). To encounter opposition twice is a true testing of the faith of the young church. It is also a test because the apostles almost meet death.

Chapter 6

8 And Stephen, full of grace and power, was doing great wonders and signs among the people. 9 Then some of those who belonged to the synagogue of the Freedmen (as it was called), and of the

---

3. Acts 5:17–18; Acts 5:27–33; Acts 5:40.

Appendix

> Cyrenians, and of the Alexandrians, and of those from Cilicia and Asia, rose up and disputed with Stephen. 10 But they could not withstand the wisdom and the Spirit with which he was speaking. 11 Then they secretly instigated men who said, "We have heard him speak blasphemous words against Moses and God." 12 And they stirred up the people and the elders and the scribes, and they came upon him and seized him and brought him before the council, 13 and they set up false witnesses who said, "This man never ceases to speak words against this holy place and the law, 14 for we have heard him say that this Jesus of Nazareth will destroy this place and will change the customs that Moses delivered to us."[4]

Note: Stephen, filled with the Spirit, continues the apostolic practice of doing wonders, causing leaders in the synagogue to dispute with him. This escalation of conflict results in false accusations by these Jews toward Stephen. He is then seized and brought before the Jewish council to answer the accusations of false witnesses.

Chapter 7

> 54 Now when they heard these things they were enraged, and they ground their teeth at him. 55 But he, full of the Holy Spirit, gazed into heaven and saw the glory of God, and Jesus standing at the right hand of God. 56 And he said, "Behold, I see the heavens opened, and the Son of Man standing at the right hand of God." 57 But they cried out with a loud voice and stopped their ears and rushed together at him. 58 Then they cast him out of the city and stoned him. And the witnesses laid down their garments at the feet of a young man named Saul. 59 And as they were stoning Stephen, he called out, "Lord Jesus, receive my spirit." 60 And falling to his knees he cried out with a loud voice, "Lord, do not hold this sin against them." And when he had said this, he fell asleep. 1 And Saul approved of his execution.[5]

Note: After preaching a sermon before the Jewish council, one in which Stephen lays out God's "progress of redemption" and traces the resistance of God's people toward the work of the Holy Spirit, rather than responding in repentance, they ironically resist Stephen's message and stone him to death in acts of rage (Persecution #3).

---

4. Acts 6:8–14.
5. Acts 7:54–8:1a.

Appendix

Chapter 8

"And there arose on that day a great persecution against the church in Jerusalem, and they were all scattered throughout the regions of Judea and Samaria, except the apostles."[6]

Note: After Stephen's martyrdom, and along with Saul's approval, the church in Jerusalem becomes subject to a full scale Jewish persecution, thus scattering the majority of the believers out of the city of Jerusalem (Persecution #4).

Chapter 9

But Saul, still breathing threats and murder against the disciples of the Lord, went to the high priest 2 and asked him for letters to the synagogues at Damascus, so that if he found any belonging to the Way, men or women, he might bring them bound to Jerusalem.

... 22 But Saul increased all the more in strength, and confounded the Jews who lived in Damascus by proving that Jesus was the Christ. 23 When many days had passed, the Jews plotted to kill him, 24 but their plot became known to Saul. They were watching the gates day and night in order to kill him, 25 but his disciples took him by night and let him down through an opening in the wall, lowering him in a basket.[7]

Note: Saul's conversion to Christ and his immediate ministry to his own people, the Jews, causes much contention and actually leads to a threat of death for the Apostle. Like Christ, Saul came to his own people first and his own people did not receive his message, one that points to Christ.

Chapter 10

44 While Peter was still saying these things, the Holy Spirit fell on all who heard the word. 45 And the believers from among the circumcised who had come with Peter were amazed, because the gift of the Holy Spirit was poured out even on the Gentiles. 46 For they were hearing them speaking in tongues and extolling God. Then Peter declared, 47 "Can anyone withhold water for baptizing these

---

6. Acts 8:1b.
7. Acts 9:1–2; Acts 9:22–25.

people, who have received the Holy Spirit just as we have?" 48 And he commanded them to be baptized in the name of Jesus Christ. Then they asked him to remain for some days.[8]

Note: The scene of the book of Acts shifts from the pursuit of the Jews with the gospel to the open door of the gospel with the Gentiles. Peter, accompanied by a group of other Jewish believers, watches God pour out his Holy Spirit upon the Gentiles. The transition from Jewish evangelism to world-wide evangelism is almost complete.

Chapter 11

15 As I began to speak, the Holy Spirit fell on them just as on us at the beginning. 16 And I remembered the word of the Lord, how he said, 'John baptized with water, but you will be baptized with the Holy Spirit.' 17 If then God gave the same gift to them as he gave to us when we believed in the Lord Jesus Christ, who was I that I could stand in God's way?" 18 When they heard these things they fell silent. And they glorified God, saying, "Then to the Gentiles also God has granted repentance that leads to life." 19 Now those who were scattered because of the persecution that arose over Stephen traveled as far as Phoenicia and Cyprus and Antioch, speaking the word to no one except Jews.[9]

Note: Peter recounts and acknowledges the reality that the God of Israel is pursuing the Gentiles. Luke writes a reminder that originally, when Jewish persecution broke out against the Jewish church in Jerusalem, those scattered believers focused upon taking God's word to Jews only. It is implied that this scenario is about to change significantly.

Chapter 12

About that time Herod the king laid violent hands on some who belonged to the church. 2 He killed James the brother of John with the sword, 3 and when he saw that it pleased the Jews, he proceeded to arrest Peter also. This was during the days of Unleavened Bread. 4 And when he had seized him, he put him in prison, delivering him over to four squads of soldiers to guard him, intending after the Passover to bring him out to the people. 5 So Peter was

8. Acts 10:44–48.
9. Acts 11:15–19.

Appendix

kept in prison, but earnest prayer for him was made to God by the church.[10]

Note: King Herod (Agrippa), who often sympathized with the Jews, attacks the Jerusalem church and its leaders, killing James and arresting Peter. Peter is rescued from prison by an angel of the Lord and survives Herod's Jewish-influenced bad behavior.

Chapter 13

4 So, being sent out by the Holy Spirit, they went down to Seleucia, and from there they sailed to Cyprus. 5 When they arrived at Salamis, they proclaimed the word of God in the synagogues of the Jews.

. . . 13 Now Paul and his companions set sail from Paphos and came to Perga in Pamphylia. And John left them and returned to Jerusalem, 14 but they went on from Perga and came to Antioch in Pisidia. And on the Sabbath day they went into the synagogue and sat down. 15 After the reading from the Law and the Prophets, the rulers of the synagogue sent a message to them, saying, "Brothers, if you have any word of encouragement for the people, say it."

. . . 42 As they went out, the people begged that these things might be told them the next Sabbath. 43 And after the meeting of the synagogue broke up, many Jews and devout converts to Judaism followed Paul and Barnabas, who, as they spoke with them, urged them to continue in the grace of God. 44 The next Sabbath almost the whole city gathered to hear the word of the Lord. 45 But when the Jews saw the crowds, they were filled with jealousy and began to contradict what was spoken by Paul, reviling him. 46 And Paul and Barnabas spoke out boldly, saying, "It was necessary that the word of God be spoken first to you. Since you thrust it aside and judge yourselves unworthy of eternal life, behold, we are turning to the Gentiles. 47 For so the Lord has commanded us, saying, "'I have made you a light for the Gentiles, that you may bring salvation to the ends of the earth.'" 48 And when the Gentiles heard this, they began rejoicing and glorifying the word of the Lord, and as many as were appointed to eternal life believed. 49 And the word of the Lord was spreading throughout the whole region. 50 But the Jews incited the devout women of high standing and the leading men of the city, stirred up persecution against Paul and Barnabas,

---

10. Acts 12:1–5.

and drove them out of their district. 51 But they shook off the dust from their feet against them and went to Iconium. 52 And the disciples were filled with joy and with the Holy Spirit.[11]

Note: In the Apostle Paul's first missionary journey, he goes directly to the synagogue in order to tell the Jews of Salamis, on the island of Cyprus, about the work of God. He does the same in Antioch of Pisidia, where the missionary team gains quite a following, so much so that Luke writes that the following week almost the entire city turns out to hear the message. However, jealous Jews contradict Paul and revile him. Paul recognizes that this is the moment to clarify the worldwide thrust of God's redemptive plan. Paul's declaration, "For so the Lord has commanded us, saying, 'I have made you a light for the Gentiles, that you may bring salvation to the ends of the earth'" states the pivotal turn that gospel proclamation is about to take. Many respond in the region, but the Jews incite local women and men to drive the apostles out of the city. Although the Jewish synagogue will remain a strategic location for the Apostle to use in his outreach, the huge mission field of the Gentiles becomes his primary focus.

Chapter 14

Now at Iconium they entered together into the Jewish synagogue and spoke in such a way that a great number of both Jews and Greeks believed. 2 But the unbelieving Jews stirred up the Gentiles and poisoned their minds against the brothers. 3 So they remained for a long time, speaking boldly for the Lord, who bore witness to the word of his grace, granting signs and wonders to be done by their hands. 4 But the people of the city were divided; some sided with the Jews and some with the apostles. 5 When an attempt was made by both Gentiles and Jews, with their rulers, to mistreat them and to stone them, 6 they learned of it and fled to Lystra and Derbe, cities of Lycaonia, and to the surrounding country, 7 and there they continued to preach the gospel.

. . . 19 But Jews came from Antioch and Iconium, and having persuaded the crowds, they stoned Paul and dragged him out of the city, supposing that he was dead. 20 But when the disciples gathered about him, he rose up and entered the city, and on the next day he went on with Barnabas to Derbe. 21 When they had preached the gospel to that city and had made many disciples, they

---

11. Acts 13:4–5; Acts 13:13–15; Acts 13:42–52.

returned to Lystra and to Iconium and to Antioch, 22 strengthening the souls of the disciples, encouraging them to continue in the faith, and saying that through many tribulations we must enter the kingdom of God.[12]

Note: As is their practice, Paul and his companions enter the synagogue at Iconium, where we are told that both Jews and Gentiles believe. However, unbelieving Jews stir up resistance and upon the threat of being stoned, the disciples flee for their lives and preach elsewhere. Sadly, these persistent unbelievers follow Paul, stone him, and almost kill him. He survives and his ministry continues. Some Jewish receptivity continues to occur, but Jewish contention and persecution will remain a staple of Paul's gospel ministry in the future.

Chapter 15

But some men came down from Judea and were teaching the brothers, "Unless you are circumcised according to the custom of Moses, you cannot be saved." 2 And after Paul and Barnabas had no small dissension and debate with them, Paul and Barnabas and some of the others were appointed to go up to Jerusalem to the apostles and the elders about this question. 3 So, being sent on their way by the church, they passed through both Phoenicia and Samaria, describing in detail the conversion of the Gentiles, and brought great joy to all the brothers. 4 When they came to Jerusalem, they were welcomed by the church and the apostles and the elders, and they declared all that God had done with them. 5 But some believers who belonged to the party of the Pharisees rose up and said, "It is necessary to circumcise them and to order them to keep the law of Moses." 6 The apostles and the elders were gathered together to consider this matter. 7 And after there had been much debate, Peter stood up and said to them, "Brothers, you know that in the early days God made a choice among you, that by my mouth the Gentiles should hear the word of the gospel and believe. 8 And God, who knows the heart, bore witness to them, by giving them the Holy Spirit just as he did to us, 9 and he made no distinction between us and them, having cleansed their hearts by faith. 10 Now, therefore, why are you putting God to the test by placing a yoke on the neck of the disciples that neither our fathers nor we have been able to bear? 11 But we believe that we

---

12. Acts 14:1–7; Acts 14:19–22.

will be saved through the grace of the Lord Jesus, just as they will." 12 And all the assembly fell silent, and they listened to Barnabas and Paul as they related what signs and wonders God had done through them among the Gentiles. 13 After they finished speaking, James replied, "Brothers, listen to me. 14 Simeon has related how God first visited the Gentiles, to take from them a people for his name. 15 And with this the words of the prophets agree, just as it is written, 16 "'After this I will return, and I will rebuild the tent of David that has fallen; I will rebuild its ruins, and I will restore it, 17 that the remnant of mankind may seek the Lord, and all the Gentiles who are called by my name, says the Lord, who makes these things 18 known from of old.'"[13]

Note: Simply stated, this chapter is a major one in the shift from the evangelization of the Jews to the inclusion of the Gentiles into God's kingdom. Both Jewish legalism and hesitancy to receive the Gentiles is addressed and resolved. The Gentiles are in!

Chapter 17

Now when they had passed through Amphipolis and Apollonia, they came to Thessalonica, where there was a synagogue of the Jews. 2 And Paul went in, as was his custom, and on three Sabbath days he reasoned with them from the Scriptures, 3 explaining and proving that it was necessary for the Christ to suffer and to rise from the dead, and saying, "This Jesus, whom I proclaim to you, is the Christ." 4 And some of them were persuaded and joined Paul and Silas, as did a great many of the devout Greeks and not a few of the leading women. 5 But the Jews were jealous, and taking some wicked men of the rabble, they formed a mob, set the city in an uproar, and attacked the house of Jason, seeking to bring them out to the crowd. 6 And when they could not find them, they dragged Jason and some of the brothers before the city authorities, shouting, "These men who have turned the world upside down have come here also, 7 and Jason has received them, and they are all acting against the decrees of Caesar, saying that there is another king, Jesus." 8 And the people and the city authorities were disturbed when they heard these things. 9 And when they had taken money as security from Jason and the rest, they let them go.

---

13. Acts 15:1–18.

Appendix

> ... 10 The brothers immediately sent Paul and Silas away by night to Berea, and when they arrived they went into the Jewish synagogue. 11 Now these Jews were more noble than those in Thessalonica; they received the word with all eagerness, examining the Scriptures daily to see if these things were so. 12 Many of them therefore believed, with not a few Greek women of high standing as well as men. 13 But when the Jews from Thessalonica learned that the word of God was proclaimed by Paul at Berea also, they came there too, agitating and stirring up the crowds. 14 Then the brothers immediately sent Paul off on his way to the sea, but Silas and Timothy remained there.
>
> ... 16 Now while Paul was waiting for them at Athens, his spirit was provoked within him as he saw that the city was full of idols. 17 So he reasoned in the synagogue with the Jews and the devout persons, and in the marketplace every day with those who happened to be there. 18 Some of the Epicurean and Stoic philosophers also conversed with him.[14]

Note: Paul continues to use his strategy of entering synagogues as a touchpoint for proclaiming Christ. He goes to the synagogue in Thessalonica, where some Jews believe, along with some Gentiles and some significant women. He also goes to the synagogue at Berea and in Athens. Sadly, in Thessalonica, jealous Jews form an oppressive mob and Paul and Silas must leave the city. This departure leads them to the city of Berea where once again, their ministry is well received and the Berean Jews of the synagogue believe. But Jews from Thessalonica follow Paul and stir up the crowds against the missionary team, forcing Paul, once again, to leave. In Athens, Paul evangelizes both Jews of the synagogue and those in the marketplace.

Chapter 18

> 5 When Silas and Timothy arrived from Macedonia, Paul was occupied with the word, testifying to the Jews that the Christ was Jesus. 6 And when they opposed and reviled him, he shook out his garments and said to them, "Your blood be on your own heads! I am innocent. From now on I will go to the Gentiles." 7 And he left there and went to the house of a man named Titius Justus, a worshiper of God. His house was next door to the synagogue. 8 Crispus, the ruler of the synagogue, believed in the Lord, together with

---

14. Acts 17:1–9; Acts 17:10–14; Acts 17:16–18.

Appendix

his entire household. And many of the Corinthians hearing Paul believed and were baptized. 9 And the Lord said to Paul one night in a vision, "Do not be afraid, but go on speaking and do not be silent, 10 for I am with you, and no one will attack you to harm you, for I have many in this city who are my people." 11 And he stayed a year and six months, teaching the word of God among them.

... 18 After this, Paul stayed many days longer and then took leave of the brothers and set sail for Syria, and with him Priscilla and Aquila. At Cenchreae he had cut his hair, for he was under a vow. 19 And they came to Ephesus, and he left them there, but he himself went into the synagogue and reasoned with the Jews. 20 When they asked him to stay for a longer period, he declined. 21 But on taking leave of them he said, "I will return to you if God wills," and he set sail from Ephesus.[15]

Note: In this text, we not only see Paul, in the midst of Jewish opposition, telling the Jews that God has ordained him to go to the Gentiles (Acts 9:15), but with a sense of exasperation, he shakes out his garment, washes his hands of their judgment (blood), and resolves to spend his efforts evangelizing the Gentiles. Paul will continue to proclaim the gospel in the synagogue, but he will also continue to meet resistance and unbelief from the majority of his Jewish audiences.

Chapter 19

"And he entered the synagogue and for three months spoke boldly, reasoning and persuading them about the kingdom of God. 9 But when some became stubborn and continued in unbelief, speaking evil of the Way before the congregation, he withdrew from them and took the disciples with him, reasoning daily in the hall of Tyrannus. 10 This continued for two years, so that all the residents of Asia heard the word of the Lord, both Jews and Greeks."[16]

Note: Although washing his hands of the blood of the Jews, who have rejected his ministry and message, Paul continues to do "synagogue evangelism" while in Ephesus. He also continues to experience a response of unbelief, and these Jews even speak evil of this new religion known as "the

---

15. Acts 18:5–11; Acts 18:18–21.
16. Acts 19:8–10.

Appendix

Way." Paul withdraws from these recalcitrant Jews and takes his ministry elsewhere.

Chapter 20

After the uproar ceased, Paul sent for the disciples, and after encouraging them, he said farewell and departed for Macedonia. 2 When he had gone through those regions and had given them much encouragement, he came to Greece. 3 There he spent three months, and when a plot was made against him by the Jews as he was about to set sail for Syria, he decided to return through Macedonia.

. . . 17 Now from Miletus he sent to Ephesus and called the elders of the church to come to him. 18 And when they came to him, he said to them: "You yourselves know how I lived among you the whole time from the first day that I set foot in Asia, 19 serving the Lord with all humility and with tears and with trials that happened to me through the plots of the Jews; 20 how I did not shrink from declaring to you anything that was profitable, and teaching you in public and from house to house, 21 testifying both to Jews and to Greeks of repentance toward God and of faith in our Lord Jesus Christ.[17]

Note: Just as God's people attacked God's prophets in the Old Testament, and eventually attack God's Son, Jesus, thus crucifying him, the Jews of Greece make plots against the life of God's Apostle, Paul.

Chapter 21

7 When we had finished the voyage from Tyre, we arrived at Ptolemais, and we greeted the brothers and stayed with them for one day. 8 On the next day we departed and came to Caesarea, and we entered the house of Philip the evangelist, who was one of the seven, and stayed with him. 9 He had four unmarried daughters, who prophesied. 10 While we were staying for many days, a prophet named Agabus came down from Judea. 11 And coming to us, he took Paul's belt and bound his own feet and hands and said, "Thus says the Holy Spirit, 'This is how the Jews at Jerusalem will bind the man who owns this belt and deliver him into

---

17. Acts 20:1–3; Acts 20:17–21.

Appendix

the hands of the Gentiles.'" 12 When we heard this, we and the people there urged him not to go up to Jerusalem. 13 Then Paul answered, "What are you doing, weeping and breaking my heart? For I am ready not only to be imprisoned but even to die in Jerusalem for the name of the Lord Jesus." 14 And since he would not be persuaded, we ceased and said, "Let the will of the Lord be done."[18]

Note: The threat of Jewish persecution remains and it is highlighted by a prophet named Agabus. The Jews, just as with Jesus, will deliver the Apostle into the hands of the Gentiles. Paul continues to assert that his gospel of repentance and faith is focused upon both Jews (mentioned first) and Greeks. He still wants the Jews to hear about their messiah and to both believe in and turn to him.

Chapter 22

17 When I had returned to Jerusalem and was praying in the temple, I fell into a trance 18 and saw him saying to me, 'Make haste and get out of Jerusalem quickly, because they will not accept your testimony about me.' 19 And I said, 'Lord, they themselves know that in one synagogue after another I imprisoned and beat those who believed in you. 20 And when the blood of Stephen your witness was being shed, I myself was standing by and approving and watching over the garments of those who killed him.' 21 And he said to me, 'Go, for I will send you far away to the Gentiles.'" 22 Up to this word they listened to him. Then they raised their voices and said, "Away with such a fellow from the earth! For he should not be allowed to live." 23 And as they were shouting and throwing off their cloaks and flinging dust into the air, 24 the tribune ordered him to be brought into the barracks, saying that he should be examined by flogging, to find out why they were shouting against him like this. 25 But when they had stretched him out for the whips, Paul said to the centurion who was standing by, "Is it lawful for you to flog a man who is a Roman citizen and uncondemned?"[19]

Note: During Paul's final visit to Jerusalem, he has an astounding opportunity to speak to the local Jews there one more time. He explains his Jewish background, gives his personal testimony of faith in Christ, and elaborates

---

18. Acts 21:7–14.
19. Acts 22:17–25.

on his God-ordained call to take Christ to the Gentiles. At that point, hearing his Jewish sympathy for the Gentiles, the furor that erupts is so great that the Roman guards suspect that he is an agitator and possible rebel. He has been handed over by the Jews to the Gentiles, just as Agabus had earlier predicted.

Chapter 23

> 12 When it was day, the Jews made a plot and bound themselves by an oath neither to eat nor drink till they had killed Paul. 13 There were more than forty who made this conspiracy. 14 They went to the chief priests and elders and said, "We have strictly bound ourselves by an oath to taste no food till we have killed Paul. 15 Now therefore you, along with the council, give notice to the tribune to bring him down to you, as though you were going to determine his case more exactly. And we are ready to kill him before he comes near."[20]

Note: Paul's gospel message is so reprehensible to the Jewish community that, ironically, a group of Jews plot to put him to death, just as the Pharisees and Sadducees had done with Jesus. Paul indeed has been called to suffer for the name of Christ (Acts 9:15).

Chapter 24

> And after five days the high priest Ananias came down with some elders and a spokesman, one Tertullus. They laid before the governor their case against Paul. 2 And when he had been summoned, Tertullus began to accuse him, saying: "Since through you we enjoy much peace, and since by your foresight, most excellent Felix, reforms are being made for this nation, 3 in every way and everywhere we accept this with all gratitude. 4 But, to detain you no further, I beg you in your kindness to hear us briefly. 5 For we have found this man a plague, one who stirs up riots among all the Jews throughout the world and is a ringleader of the sect of the Nazarenes. 6 He even tried to profane the temple, but we seized him. 8 By examining him yourself you will be able to find out from him about everything of which we accuse him." 9 The Jews also joined in the charge, affirming that all these things were so.

---

20. Acts 23:12–15.

Appendix

> ... 24 After some days Felix came with his wife Drusilla, who was Jewish, and he sent for Paul and heard him speak about faith in Christ Jesus. 25 And as he reasoned about righteousness and self-control and the coming judgment, Felix was alarmed and said, "Go away for the present. When I get an opportunity I will summon you." 26 At the same time he hoped that money would be given him by Paul. So he sent for him often and conversed with him. 27 When two years had elapsed, Felix was succeeded by Porcius Festus. And desiring to do the Jews a favor, Felix left Paul in prison.[21]

Note: Luke enumerates the many accusations that the Jews have constructed against Paul. Jewish antagonism toward Paul is extremely high, such that, any accusation, even if patently false, is affirmed. The Jewish hostility toward Paul is so great that Felix, ignoring justice, appeases the Jews to the detriment of Paul's well-being.

Chapter 25

> Now three days after Festus had arrived in the province, he went up to Jerusalem from Caesarea. 2 And the chief priests and the principal men of the Jews laid out their case against Paul, and they urged him, 3 asking as a favor against Paul that he summon him to Jerusalem—because they were planning an ambush to kill him on the way. 4 Festus replied that Paul was being kept at Caesarea and that he himself intended to go there shortly. 5 "So," said he, "let the men of authority among you go down with me, and if there is anything wrong about the man, let them bring charges against him." 6 After he stayed among them not more than eight or ten days, he went down to Caesarea. And the next day he took his seat on the tribunal and ordered Paul to be brought. 7 When he had arrived, the Jews who had come down from Jerusalem stood around him, bringing many and serious charges against him that they could not prove. 8 Paul argued in his defense, "Neither against the law of the Jews, nor against the temple, nor against Caesar have I committed any offense." 9 But Festus, wishing to do the Jews a favor, said to Paul, "Do you wish to go up to Jerusalem and there be tried on these charges before me?" 10 But Paul said, "I am standing before Caesar's tribunal, where I ought to be tried. To the Jews I have done no wrong, as you yourself know very well. 11 If then I am a wrongdoer and have committed anything for which I deserve to

---

21. Acts 24:1–9; Acts 24:24–27.

Appendix

die, I do not seek to escape death. But if there is nothing to their charges against me, no one can give me up to them. I appeal to Caesar." 12 Then Festus, when he had conferred with his council, answered, "To Caesar you have appealed; to Caesar you shall go."[22]

Note: While imprisoned for almost two years, Jews continue to "lurk," waiting for an opportunity to disparage and condemn the Apostle Paul. Luke builds a subtle case for Paul's innocence with regard to Jewish law and practice, but also explains that it is the Jewish persecution that has generated Paul's deliverance from their antagonism and his consequential travels to Rome.

Chapter 26

So Agrippa said to Paul, "You have permission to speak for yourself." Then Paul stretched out his hand and made his defense: 2 "I consider myself fortunate that it is before you, King Agrippa, I am going to make my defense today against all the accusations of the Jews, 3 especially because you are familiar with all the customs and controversies of the Jews. Therefore I beg you to listen to me patiently. 4 "My manner of life from my youth, spent from the beginning among my own nation and in Jerusalem, is known by all the Jews. 5 They have known for a long time, if they are willing to testify, that according to the strictest party of our religion I have lived as a Pharisee. 6 And now I stand here on trial because of my hope in the promise made by God to our fathers, 7 to which our twelve tribes hope to attain, as they earnestly worship night and day. And for this hope I am accused by Jews, O king! 8 Why is it thought incredible by any of you that God raises the dead?

. . . 12 In this connection I journeyed to Damascus with the authority and commission of the chief priests. 13 At midday, O king, I saw on the way a light from heaven, brighter than the sun, that shone around me and those who journeyed with me. 14 And when we had all fallen to the ground, I heard a voice saying to me in the Hebrew language, 'Saul, Saul, why are you persecuting me? It is hard for you to kick against the goads.' 15 And I said, 'Who are you, Lord?' And the Lord said, 'I am Jesus whom you are persecuting. 16 But rise and stand upon your feet, for I have appeared to you for this purpose, to appoint you as a servant and witness to the things in which you have seen me and to those in which I will

22. Acts 25:1–12.

Appendix

appear to you, 17 delivering you from your people and from the Gentiles—to whom I am sending you 18 to open their eyes, so that they may turn from darkness to light and from the power of Satan to God, that they may receive forgiveness of sins and a place among those who are sanctified by faith in me.'[23]

Note: Due to Jewish opposition and Paul's subsequent imprisonment, Paul is able to preach the gospel to King Agrippa (the King of Judea), and to declare the truth of the resurrection. Paul is able to tell this high authority figure that his calling from Christ is to proclaim the forgiveness of sins to both the Jews and the Gentiles, leading both out of darkness into light.

Chapter 28

17 After three days he called together the local leaders of the Jews, and when they had gathered, he said to them, "Brothers, though I had done nothing against our people or the customs of our fathers, yet I was delivered as a prisoner from Jerusalem into the hands of the Romans. 18 When they had examined me, they wished to set me at liberty, because there was no reason for the death penalty in my case. 19 But because the Jews objected, I was compelled to appeal to Caesar—though I had no charge to bring against my nation. 20 For this reason, therefore, I have asked to see you and speak with you, since it is because of the hope of Israel that I am wearing this chain." 21 And they said to him, "We have received no letters from Judea about you, and none of the brothers coming here has reported or spoken any evil about you. 22 But we desire to hear from you what your views are, for with regard to this sect we know that everywhere it is spoken against." 23 When they had appointed a day for him, they came to him at his lodging in greater numbers. From morning till evening he expounded to them, testifying to the kingdom of God and trying to convince them about Jesus both from the Law of Moses and from the Prophets. 24 And some were convinced by what he said, but others disbelieved. 25 And disagreeing among themselves, they departed after Paul had made one statement: "The Holy Spirit was right in saying to your fathers through Isaiah the prophet:

> 26 "'Go to this people, and say,
> "You will indeed hear but never understand,
> and you will indeed see but never perceive."

---

23. Acts 26:1–8; Acts 26:12–18.

> 27 For this people's heart has grown dull,
> and with their ears they can barely hear,
> and their eyes they have closed;
> lest they should see with their eyes
> and hear with their ears
> and understand with their heart
> and turn, and I would heal them.'
>
> 28 Therefore let it be known to you that this salvation of God has been sent to the Gentiles; they will listen." 30 He lived there two whole years at his own expense, and welcomed all who came to him, 31 proclaiming the kingdom of God and teaching about the Lord Jesus Christ with all boldness and without hindrance.[24]

Note: Luke wraps up his account by demonstrating that Paul—even while under house arrest—continues to try to convince the Jews that their messiah has come. Some are convinced, but others disbelieve, justifying Paul's mission to go to the Gentiles who will listen to God's message about his son, the Lord Jesus Christ.

Postscript: The Apostle Paul addresses this great defection of Israel from the promises of God and their messiah in the book of Romans, chapters 9–11. Their unbelief is part of God's sovereign plan to include the Gentiles in his church and the Apostle Paul underscores the reality that there is hope for Israel to be saved in the future.

---

24. Acts 28:17–31.

Bibliography

Alexander, J.A. *Acts*. Edinburgh: Banner of Truth, 1963.
Bock, Darrell L. *Acts: Baker Exegetical Commentary on the New Testament*. Grand Rapids: Baker, 2007.
Bruce, F.F. *The Book of Acts*. Grand Rapids: Eerdmans, 1954.
Kistemaker, Simon. *New Testament Commentary: Acts*. Grand Rapids: Baker, 1991.
Larkin, William. *Acts: The IVP New Testament Commentary*. Downer's Grove: InterVarsity, 1995.
Marshall, I. Howard. *Acts: Tyndale New Testament Commentaries*. Grand Rapids: Eerdmans, 1980.
Waters, Guy. *The Acts of the Apostles*. Darlington, UK: Evangelical Press, 2015.

www.ingramcontent.com/pod-product-compliance
Lightning Source LLC
Chambersburg PA
CBHW072011090426
42734CB00033B/2438